MOTHER WONDERFUL'S
CHEESECAKES
AND
OTHER GOODIES

MOTHER

WONDERFUL'S

CHEESECAKES

— AND —

OTHER GOODIES

No-Fail, Surefire,
Sweet-Tooth Delights

MYRA CHANIN

An Owl Book
HENRY HOLT *and* COMPANY
New York

Library of Congress Cataloging-in-Publication Data
Chanin, Myra.
Mother Wonderful's cheesecakes and other goodies /
No-fail, surefire, sweet-tooth delights
by Myra Chanin.
—Rev. ed.
p. cm.
ISBN 0-8050-1289-3
1. Cheesecake (Cookery) 2. Desserts. I. Title.
TX773.C47 1990
641.8'653—dc20   89-24690
                                                       CIP

Henry Holt books are available at special discounts
for bulk purchases for sales promotions, premiums,
fund-raising, or educational use. Special editions
or book excerpts can also be created to specification.

For details contact:
Special Sales Director
Henry Holt and Company, Inc.
115 West 18th Street
New York, New York 10011

Revised Edition

Designed by Katy Riegel
Illustrations copyright © 1990 by Leslie Evans

Recognizing the importance of preserving the written word,
Henry Holt and Company, Inc.,
by policy, prints all of its first editions on acid-free paper. ∞

Printed in the United States of America
1 3 5 7 9 10 8 6 4 2

Mother Wonderful is a registered trademark of Myra Chanin.

TO ALVIN,
the most generous, loving, supportive husband
in the entire world . . .
this week.

Contents

Introduction:

The History
of Mother Wonderful

Call me Myra. I'm a cookbook author who's been described as a cross between Erma Bombeck and Julia Child, unfortunately not by either one of them, yet. You may have seen me dispensing sweets to the stars on TV. My specialty is cheesecake, the baked kind. I became a professional baker because I expected to be a grass widow. My husband Alvin and I were not getting along after six years of marriage, which should not have surprised me. I'd pursued him relentlessly for three years until he finally said "I do." I'd loved him much more than he'd loved me, which gave me the lower hand in our relationship.

Alvin married me because he thought I'd make a good mother, and truth to tell, behind my passion lay my desire for a breadwinner of my very own. He is a lawyer/CPA and I was permanently-entry-level-always-on-the-verge-of-losing-my-job.

After several years of running a household and raising a child, my self-esteem blossomed along with my increased competence, and I was becoming more and more uncomfortable with the mutually held beliefs that had formerly stabilized our union: that Alvin, that long-suffering saint, was supermarvy and that I was a lucky woman to have the privilege of drying his feet with my hair.

Even more unnerving than the threat of divorce was the prospect of job hunting. Is there anything more degrading than the perpetual smile required to ingratiate oneself with a future employer? Alas, the openings available to an English major with a spotty employment record hardly coincided with my fantasies. I was offered positions as a substitute teacher when in my heart I knew I deserved to be ruler of the world.

Since I didn't take instruction well, I knew I'd have to become self-employed, and the road to independence led through my kitchen. I was an excellent cook and a decent baker, even though I avoided egg whites. (I could never determine when they were firm-but-not-stiff, and the machinations required to fold them into batter frightened me, so my hands turned into hooves and my tortes turned into pancakes.) But cooking meant working in someone else's kitchen. Baking at home would enslave me less, and there was a need for dessert makers at that time in my home town.

Philadelphia was then in the throes of a restaurant renaissance. Lots of fine young chefs had managed to open small dining rooms on a shoestring. They could barely pay the rent, let alone hire a full-time baker. I supplied desserts to these brand-new restaurateurs.

I had been lunching at Philadelphia's Fish Market, which eventually became a large, nationally lauded gourmet restaurant, but then it seated twenty at five tables in the rear. I told the owner I made a better cheesecake than the one he served. He said, "Show me." If he agreed, he'd buy them from me.

I presented him with my first creation, flavored with chutzpah. He bounced it for being too dense. The brute actually claimed it gave him heartburn! However, those years of wooing Alvin had taught me that No! didn't mean Never! So, like Robert Bruce, I returned to my mixer to try and try again. The Fish Marketeer loved the lime-almond cheesecake I brought him the following week. So did his customers. Voilà! an entrepreneur was born.

Alvin gave my new venture his all. He gained twenty pounds as my flavoring consultant and swallowed sweets until his gums dissolved. He also became my part-time delivery person, and rushed off to federal court with a briefcase in one hand and a shopping bag filled with cheesecakes in the other.

Soon more restaurateurs began knocking on my door and I branched out into more complex cakes and cookies. I dazzled clients with exotic flavors: ginger pear, mocha blanca, honey fig. Naming the cakes properly was three-fourths of the battle. My products won Philly's Best awards, and for the first time I felt like somebody wonderful—Mother Wonderful—a woman who could support herself well doing work she enjoyed in case (God forbid) she had to.

As business thrived, optimism constantly conquered prudence. I invested my profits in expensive professional equipment, a top-of-the-line food processor and the best electric mixer money could buy. The wire whip on the latter laid to rest my terror of egg whites. As my baking repertoire expanded, so did my waistline. In Mother Wonderful's kitchen, batter was wiped from fingers by human lips—mine.

I shrugged off clients' bankruptcies. Did I have any alternative? On the lists of creditors Mother Wonderful was usually preceded by the Mellon Bank. But even more distressing than their accounting legerdemain was the emotional insecurity of the restaurateurs. Right after rave reviews of some unusual goodie had encouraged me to stock up on an obscure ingredient for which there was no other earthly use, the owner's Aunt Minnie would decide that very cake was just too rich, and bingo, it was canceled. How can a cake be too rich? The same way a bride can be too beautiful. I still have several quarts of raspberry flavoring in the back of my basement.

After hiding from the Board of Health for several years and watching my weight climb up, up, and away, I passed on my clients to other underground bakers and tried my hand at writing about food. I was lucky. Philadelphia readers seemed to enjoy the way I blended chuckles and calories. Mother Wonderful went on computer.

While I was trying to sell a book of essays, a New York editor tasted one of my cheesecakes, and called me, waving money. *Mother Wonderful's Cheesecakes and Other Goodies* was first published in 1982 and sold like cheesecakes. It also got me a regular slot on national TV and celebrity status in my neighborhood, as well as recognition from Uncle Sam in 1986, when Mother Wonderful became a registered trademark.

Working with Gary Collins on "Hour Magazine" was the icing on the cake. To my delight, I've proven that you don't have to be young, pretty, and skinny to become a television personality, but thanks to a Jose Eber beauty makeover on "Hour Magazine" I got more attractive and more vain as I grew older.

Did my marriage collapse? No. It's actually thriving! Alvin and I are billing and cooing after twenty-three years, quite a feat in times when folks discard mates as casually as they dispose of paper plates. Did cheesecake keep my marriage together? It didn't hurt it. It's impossible for anyone who enjoys fine food to stay mad at the hand that feeds him. Alvin may want to get away from me from time to time, but he'll never desert my desserts. Besides, I have convinced him that I'm not a good sport. He knows he will pay dearly for his lithe, lovely tootsie. Alvin is an acquisitive man who loves his possessions. He will make almost any sacrifice rather than lose half of his assets.

If you want to get or stay married, good food is a tried and tested route. I know that relationships are supposed to be equal, but the classic approach to connubial bliss has always been 50 percent culinary. The reason everyone says the way to a man's heart is through his stomach is because we all know that it isn't through his brains. Soft lights, sweet music, and diaphanous gowns may create an evening's diversion, but comes the dawn and even Casanova must eat. The sensuous woman who serves a sensuous cheesecake will always have men lined up outside her door. Besides, a little cheesecake never hurt anybody. Those heavy cream sauces in French bistros turn cardiovascular surgeons into millionaires.

If the man in your life likes to eat, he'll cleave to you forever, because a few years down the line, when he finds himself with time on his hands, indiscretionary income in his wallet, and a craving in his loins for tall, blonde stewardae, he'll probably get a C- on his stress tests and will once again appreciate a loyal wifey with equal amounts of compassion, cellulite, and culinary skills, which include a wicked way with oat bran. Remember, the mature male is more attractive to younger women proffering the Gold Card in a dimly lit disco than waving the Blue Cross Card in a brightly antiseptic ICU.

Sex has limitations. Desserts are infinitely more versatile and far easier to duplicate than those weird positions in *The Joy of Sex*. Besides, sex goddesses have trouble holding on to their men. Remember how many lovers deserted Marilyn Monroe. Can you imagine any man ever tiring of the infinite variety of Julia Child?

MOTHER WONDERFUL'S
CHEESECAKES
AND
OTHER GOODIES

Choices

My grandmother taught me that the three most important elements of cooking were ingredients, ingredients, and ingredients. Even in the middle of the Great Depression, she always turned up her nose at the feature of the week and asked all of her food purveyors the same question. "Do you have for more money?"

After they displayed the cream of their wares, she always asked them a second question, "How much?" and then always gave the same reply to their reply. "Are you crazy? You want me to take out a mortgage to buy a pound of top rib?" But everyone knew she was going to buy the high-priced spread and they began to bargain in earnest to determine what price she'd pay.

Those kinds of relationships are hard to establish with a supermarket clerk, and since the owners, Robert Acme or Sam Pathmark, are seldom on the premises, I can't go eyeball to eyeball with them. But I do believe that quality costs more. I often prefer imports, and I would advise you to follow my lead.

To give you the benefit of my experience, I'm going to recommend some of my favorites here. For crumb crusts, I prefer Nabisco Nilla Wafers because they grind up very finely. I also think Nabisco's Famous Chocolate Wafers are the absolute tops. Unfortunately both are off-limits for kosher cooks, who could substitute Nabisco's Brown

Edge Wafers for the Nilla Wafers and any Pepperidge Farm chocolate cookie for the Famous Chocolate Wafers.

For baked cheesecakes, I prefer sweet chocolate. That designation doesn't mean that the chocolate has an exceptional amount of sugar in it. It merely means that it contains a higher ratio of cocoa and is thus more dense. My favorite is Maillard Eagle Sweet Chocolate, but I also find Baker's quite acceptable and it's easier to procure.

As for sugar itself, I recommend the superfine, sometimes called "bar" sugar because it dissolves instantly even in cool liquids. It completely eliminates graininess, especially in the sour cream glaze. Domino makes one called Pure Cane Superfine Dessert Sugar. All measurements for superfine sugar are exactly the same as for granulated.

Don't look for bargains in cream cheese. The fewer additives, the better the flavor. I've tried many of the no-frills store label brands and I generally find them mushy and gummy. I've been very satisfied with the Philadelphia-brand cream cheese. You can see the difference when you remove the foil wrapper. The block of cream cheese keeps its shape. Fleur de Lait brand is even purer. It's produced in Pennsylvania and is available nationally.

If you do not like working with big, cold blocks of cream cheese (although I can't imagine why not!), you can warm them to a delightfully workable texture in the microwave. Thirty seconds on a Medium setting softens eight ounces of cream cheese in a bowl.

Remember, the high road to imaginative cheesecakes is paved with *natural* flavorings and extracts. I'm always looking for them, no matter where I may be. Most people leave Harrod's in London with adornments for their bodies. In 1985 I ignored all the fashions on sale the day after Christmas and walked out with an entire line of extracts I'd never seen anywhere else, even though they were definitely not on sale.

In the States, McCormick natural flavors and extracts come in almond, anise, lemon, orange, peppermint, pineapple, and sherry, are available in 1-ounce bottles at many supermarkets, and sell for varying prices from $1.31 to $1.91.

Wagner extracts in adorable little 1½-ounce bottles include almond, anise, banana, black walnut, butter, rum butter, butterscotch, caramel, cherry, chocolate, cinnamon, ginger, lemon, lime, maple, mocha, orange, peppermint, pineapple, raspberry, rum, spearmint, strawberry, and wintergreen. They sell for $1.99 in gourmet and specialty food shops.

The most phenomenal selection of natural flavors and extracts comes from Bickford in Akron, Ohio, which has been in business since 1914 and went national in 1980. Here's their list:

almond	coffee	peach
amaretto	cranberry	peanut butter
anise	date	pear
apple	eggnog	peppermint
apricot	gin	pineapple
banana	ginger	pistachio
blackberry	grape	prune
black walnut	grapefruit	raisin
blueberry	guava	root beer
brandy	hazelnut	rum
butter	Irish cream	rum raisin
butter pecan	Kahlúa	scotch
butterscotch	kiwi fruit	sherry
caramel	lemon	spearmint
cherry (sweet)	lime	strawberry
cherry (wild)	mango	tangerine
chocolate	maple	tropical fruit
chocolate almond	maraschino	vanilla butter nut
chocolate cherry	mint	walnut
chocolate mint	nutmeg	watermelon
cinnamon	orange	wintergreen
clove	papaya	
coconut	passion fruit	

Wow!

Price:
$1.79 1-ounce bottle
$2.99 2-ounce bottle
$5.49 4-ounce bottle
$8.59 8-ounce bottle

They are available in many supermarkets, health food stores, and gourmet food shops, or you can just call Bickford toll-free at 1-800-283-8322 and ask for Steve. He's the owner. Give him your credit card number and he'll ship out whatever your heart desires by UPS.

La Torre extracts are artificial but artful. Even though they were designed as cordial and liqueur flavorings, they work well with cream cheese. Here's a list of their infinite varieties:

alkermes	cinnamon	peach
almond	cherry	peach brandy
amaretto	cherry brandy	pineapple
anesone	cognac	raspberry
anise	crema di cacao	rock and rye
anisette	crema di menta	rosolio
apricot	curaçao	Jamaica rum
apricot brandy	Galliano	rum brandy
banana	gin	rye
B & B	Goccia d'oro	Sambuca
Benedictine	Grand Marnier	slivovitz
blackberry	Kaiser pear	strawberry
blackberry brandy	kirsch	Strega
bourbon	lemon	tutti-frutti
caffè sport	mandarino	vermouth
Chartreuse	marsala	whiskey
cherry	orange	

They're priced at $1.25 per ½-ounce bottle and are available by mail from The Spice Corner, 904 South 9th Street, Philadelphia, PA 19147, (215) 925-1660. If you don't know what alkermes tastes like, rest easy. Neither do I. I'm told it is a cordial flavored with nutmeg, cinnamon, bay leaf, and cloves. One of these days when I have nothing to do, I'm going to add it to a pumpkin cheesecake.

Measurements

To help you figure out how much of what you'll need to make one cup of crumbs, here are some meaningful measurements I've made. I do recommend that you get yourself a small kitchen scale, because I think weight determinations are more consistent. You don't need a state-of-the-art wonder that tallies how many calories you swallowed while no one was looking. A small postal scale is quite adequate.

Number of Cookies Required to Produce
One Cup of Crumbs

TYPE OF COOKIE	COARSELY CHOPPED	FINELY CHOPPED
Chips Ahoy	8 cookies	11 cookies
Famous Chocolate Wafers	14 cookies	18 cookies
Graham crackers	10 crackers	14 crackers
Shortbread	13 cookies	14 cookies
Vanilla wafers	20 cookies	25 cookies
Gingersnaps	12 cookies	18 cookies
Chocolate sandwich	9 cookies	13 cookies

Nuts

For crusts, I prefer nuts chopped medium fine, which means somewhere between small chunks and nut butter. Ideal nut bits should be the size of kosher salt, and fine but fluffy. *Never chop nuts in advance and store them.* You want them as fresh as possible so they don't get oily and/or rancid and make your crust too greasy when they combine with the other ingredients in it.

You can start with either whole nuts or nut pieces/chunks in your processor. Run it for 20 seconds and then continue chopping, using the off-on pulse, and checking the texture of the nuts every 15 or 20 pulses as well as stirring them around to keep their texture consistent; otherwise some of them will turn into nut butter. Hard nuts like almonds acquire the preferred texture easily. Softer nuts like macadamia and pine nuts have to be closely watched or they mush up.

The following nut chart is direct from the horse's mouth, Planter's, but slightly modified. Since so many people buy those little packets that hang on supermarket racks, these measurements will help you buy just the amount that you need. Don't treat the measurements on the outside of the package as gospel. I reweighed and remeasured them and got slightly different results. A tablespoon or two more of chopped nuts in a crumb crust mixture adds richness to the taste and increases the volume, which decreases your fear that there won't be enough to go around.

Bagged Packages of Nuts

NUT	WEIGHT	CHOPPED MEDIUM FINE
ALMONDS		
blanched, slivered	2 ounces	1/2 cup + 1 tablespoon
blanched, whole	2 ounces	1/2 cup + 2 tablespoons
sliced, with skin	2 ounces	1/2 cup
whole, with skin	2 ounces	1/2 cup
BRAZIL NUTS		
whole	2 ounces	1/2 cup + 1 tablespoon
CASHEWS		
pieces	2 ounces	1/2 cup
HAZELNUTS (FILBERTS)		
whole, with skin	2 ounces	1/2 cup + 1 tablespoon
PEANUTS	2 ounces	1/2 cup + 2 tablespoons
PECANS		
pieces	2 ounces	1/2 cup + 1 tablespoon
MACADAMIA		
whole	2 ounces	scant 1/2 cup
PINE NUTS	2 ounces	1/2 cup
PISTACHIOS		
whole	2 ounces	1/2 cup + 1 tablespoon
WALNUTS		
black, pieces	2 ounces	scant 1/2 cup
English, pieces	2 1/2 ounces	1/2 cup + 2 tablespoons

Here is another table I designed to be used as a rule of thumb for any readers who, like me, haven't mastered fractions:

> 1 ounce nut meats = *1/4 cup chopped nuts*
> 2 ounces nut meats = *1/2 cup chopped nuts*
> 3 ounces nut meats = *3/4 cup chopped nuts*
> 4 ounces nut meats = *1 cup chopped nuts*

I weigh them, chop them, and then measure them. If I'm short, I can always grind a few more. Just be warned that 1 ounce of over-chopped nut meats gives you 2 tablespoons of nut butter, so if you have to choose between two evils, underchop rather than overchop. If you chop the nuts in your food processor *with your cookie crumbs*, you will prevent the nuts from turning mushy because the cookie crumbs will absorb the excess oil.

The Cheesecake Gospel
According to Mother Wonderful

READ BEFORE BAKING!

Cheesecake is the easiest dessert to make! How did it get such an awesome reputation? Bakers lie. When you find out how easy it is to make cheesecake, you'll stop paying $25.00 for theirs and start baking your own.

Bakers pass on anxiety-producing instructions that tell you to let your cheesecake sit in the oven after it's baked for 78 minutes with the door ajar. Utter nonsense! If the cake is done, it can go right into the fridge. If it isn't, it should be baked longer.

Even worse are those recipes that tell you to put your cheesecake pan in a pan filled with boiling water, a baking principle I think was devised by the marketing director of some pharmaceutical company to double the sales of adhesive bandages and first-aid sprays. I've never removed one of these from the oven without acquiring several blisters when hot water sloshed out of the *unterpot* and onto my forearms.

Cheesecakes should be custardlike in the middle and creamy around the edges. Why do people overbake them? Mostly because they're afraid they'll fall apart when they're shifted from the metal bottom of the springform pan onto a serving plate. On the other hand, if you're taking a cheesecake to a party or a picnic, transporting and serving it on the original metal springform bottom usually rewards you with another bottomless springform ring.

Here's how to circumvent the dual problem of overbaked cheese-cakes and bottomless pans. Before starting to bake, remove the metal bottom plate from the springform and replace it with a cardboard round of equal size that has been wrapped in a sheet of *heavy-duty* aluminum foil. Insert this foil-wrapped round in the springform and bake on it instead of on the original metal bottom. Cardboard cake rounds can be cut from a corrugated box that's lying around the house or purchased in most paper goods stores or baking supply houses. And if the round isn't a perfect fit, just trim off the excess with scissors or knife.

You can protect your oven from butter leaks simply by wrapping a second sheet of foil around the outside bottom rim of the spring-form and baking away. It's a good idea to do this even if you bake in a springform with the original metal bottom. Butter tends to leak out of them unless they are brand new.

When the cheesecake is ready to serve, remove the cake on its foil-lined round, put a paper doily under it, and place it on a tray or carry it to your destination. Baking cheesecakes on foil-wrapped rounds helps cement friendships, because your original metal bottoms don't get lost, and if they do, you know how to replace them and keep your pans viable.

The subtleties of flavoring always made Mother Wonderful's cheesecakes exceptional. Most of the following forty-two baked cheesecakes are ones that have been featured in restaurants and have won prizes through the years. Since I never want to unwrap another package of cream cheese, I pass all my secrets on to you. Every one of my cheesecakes can be stored, uncut and boxed, for seven days in the refrigerator, and they can all be frozen. Actually, I would suggest that you freeze leftovers after you've served the cake at a dinner party. The sour cream glaze on baked cheesecakes goes first. It de-velops an unappetizing yellow tinge and dries out so you don't want to eat it, although you really could. If you freeze it, the color stays creamy. It's very little trouble to cut frozen. Just use a warmed knife.

Before I go, I do want to answer the question that people ask me most. Which cheesecake is my favorite? My reply has always been the same: whichever one I happen to be eating.

Ten Commandments for Making Perfectly Baked Cheesecakes Every Time

READ BEFORE BAKING!

Thou Shalt Think Positive

Stay out of the kitchen when you're feeling guilty or distracted. Your cakes will come out either raw or burned. You'll gain fifteen pounds in a single sitting, scald and cut yourself, and end up covered with bandages from clavicle to wrist. Never bake when you're feeling depressed. Take to your bed with a trashy book or meet someone amusing for lunch. An even better remedy might be to take to your bed with someone amusing, but if you knew someone amusing to take to your bed you probably wouldn't feel so depressed.

Thou Shalt Pardon My Redundancies

I've always hated cookbooks that are designed for the convenience of the author, with instructions that make you shift from the page you're reading to a different section that contains the recipe for some part of the cake. I write for flawed folks like myself, with short attention spans, imperfect vision, and faulty memories, who *hate* flipping through cookbooks searching for parts of recipes (like ingredients for a crumb crust, for example) that were included in a preceding chapter.

Each recipe has every pertinent bit of information and almost every applicable tip. However, I do run on sometimes and offer nitty-gritty advice on procedures that really do not need to be included over and over again. These extensive explanations of procedures are included in the first recipe of each section, and I suggest you read them to determine if the detailed instructions will be useful to you.

Thou Shalt Never Bake
Cheesecakes at the Last Minute

Cheesecakes should be baked about two days before serving and allowed to mellow in the refrigerator. They will keep for at least a week refrigerated, and several months frozen.

Thou Shalt Use Professional Equipment

Throwaway aluminum containers are a no-no generally, because I don't feel they conduct heat properly.

You'll notice that I've included two methods (mixer and food processor) of making cheesecakes. By a mixer I mean a mixer with a bowl that stays stationary and beaters that move. A little hand mixer just doesn't do a good enough job whipping up cream cheese, and won't incorporate the eggs quickly enough. Good equipment costs more but lasts longer and does more. The KitchenAid mixer makes whipping egg whites a snap and makes folding them into batter a dream instead of a nightmare. I've been making cheesecakes for fifteen years on the same KitchenAid mixers, and I've never had any problems with them. If necessary (and if you find any takers), sell your body to buy a KitchenAid mixer and a good food processor, and stop struggling with appliances that were designed in 1904.

In the Beginning,
Thou Shalt Follow These Recipes Exactly

Cooking is an art, but baking is a science, so to be on the safe side, follow my recipes exactly. I assure you, they have been tested and retested.

Thou Shalt Measure Out
Ingredients Before Beginning to Bake

Never assume you have in your pantry every ingredient you'll need. Make sure you do before you start to bake.

There is nothing more detrimental to competent baking than finding that you don't have enough of or any of an essential ingredient when you're at a crucial point in the preparation. It makes you crazy, and you hysterically start looking for ways to replace whatever's missing, and you can't. If you haven't begun to mix, you can always stop without wasting anything, or switch to another recipe for which you have all the ingredients. It's also helpful, when working with a recipe you've never tried before, to measure out the ingredients, so you can better concentrate on the cooking process itself.

Thou Shalt Never Add Extracts to
Unadulterated Melted Chocolate

Extracts harden both white and dark chocolate. You must either blend the chocolate with melted butter or add it to the batter before adding extracts or liqueur. Chocolate doesn't work well with alcohol.

Thou Shalt Check Thy Oven's Temperature
with a Thermometer to Ascertain
that What Thou Seest Is Verily What
Thou Gettest

I check mine once a month. An incorrect temperature always produces either inconsistent results or absolute disasters. Last year at a party, the temperature in my oven was so crazy that I served half-raw veal pâté en croûte to seventy starving *fressers* (big eaters). Fortunately, they were brainwashed into believing I was a superb cook, so they all decided that if Myra served it half raw, it was supposed to be served half raw. They lapped everything up and complained about the dearth of seconds.

Thou Shalt Not Chintz on Ingredients

Never cut corners in the name of economy. It ain't thrifty to throw out an entire cake because it tastes awful. The cost differential between a sublime cheesecake and a third-rate one is less than three dollars. If money is a problem, make an 8-inch version and serve petite wedges, but always make sure anyone who tastes it will rave about your skill and beg for more.

Use the highest quality cheese, eggs, sour cream, and liqueurs available in your area. Find a dried-fruit-and-nut emporium that does a huge business. Their merchandise is constantly fresh. Or patronize a gourmet shop owned by a food fetishist who'd rather dump than sell anything that isn't top drawer. Of course, he/she may not be in business very long.

I can afford to purchase first-class ingredients because I refuse to look like an eye chart—that is, I never buy clothing with someone else's monogram, lest I begin to think I really am Gloria Montana or Ralph von Gucci and should be invited to Donald Trump's parties. I'm always amused by an associate of my husband's who fancies himself a gourmet yet complains about the outrageous prices of imported chocolate while driving around town in his new Rolls Royce.

Thou Shalt Always Add Eggs to Thy Batter with Thy Mixer on the Lowest Speed

When the mixer is set at high speed, too much air gets into the batter and produces an inferior consistency along with a cheesecake that develops a depression in the middle; then you need to put a bunch of cornstarchy gunk on top to disguise it. Feh!

Thou Shalt Rest Thy Cheesecake Before Thou Glazeth It

It is vital that the cake rest in the pan on the countertop for ten minutes after the initial baking and before the sour cream glaze is applied. This very essential step allows the interior of the cake to solidify without overbaking, burning, and/or cracking the exterior.

Thou Shalt Not Let Thy Cheesecake
Cool at Room Temperature

Despite what most recipes say, run your cake directly from the oven to the refrigerator or the cheesecake will develop cracks and fissures.

Thou Shalt Never Cover Thy Cheesecake with Aluminum Foil
or Plastic Wrap while It Cools in Thy Fridge

If you do, condensation will cause a lake to form on the top of your cake. Leave it in the pan uncovered initially or, if you must, cover the pan with a cardboard round that absorbs moisture. Once cheesecakes have cooled, you can put them in a covered box or just keep the round on top of the springform ring to protect them.

Thou Shalt Not Serve Thy
Cheesecake Directly from Thy Refrigerator

Always allow it to sit at room temperature for an hour or two before serving to enhance the flavoring. Cheesecake tastes more sensuous when it's not too cold. It also has to sit at room temperature for five to ten minutes before you remove it from the springform, which gives the butter in the crust an opportunity to relax its bond with the metal rim.

Thou Shalt Never Even Think About
Using Those Gunky Cornstarch Fruit Toppings
on Cheesecake!

. . . . Lest the Butterfat Fairy herself steal into your kitchen and put salt in your sugar bowl.

I hate those gunky cornstarch and fruit toppings. They remind me of the tinted plaster of Paris sushi you see in the windows of Japanese restaurants—the ones you normally avoid. Gunky toppings were designed to conceal major imperfections in OPC (Other People's Cheesecakes)—like crevasses and/or hollows usually caused by incorrect temperatures or too long a stay in the oven. OPCs are also beset with two other culinary blights—banal lemon-flavored batter and/or soggy graham cracker crusts. I can't decide which one of the above constitutes the greater gastronomical transgression. In Mother Wonderful's Cheesecakes, the cookie crusts are crunchy and the batters are full-flavored and unique. If you follow my instructions, none will have any major cracks and cavities that need to be filled and disguised. An enticingly flavored sour cream glaze (no all-vanilla ever!) adds a mysterious tang and supplies a pristine veneer.

Thou Shalt Never Defile Thy Crusts with Graham Cracker Crumbs

Why? Don't even ask.

Thou Shalt Use Thy Imagination

Don't be afraid to experiment. If the results aren't perfect, not to worry. As long as it's sweet, somebody in your household will eat it all up. If an ingredient intrigues you, go for it, and try to develop flavors of your own. If you make one that's outstanding, send the recipe to me and I'll give you credit and include it in the next printing of this book.

Hem, hem, you may have noticed that I am a few commandments up on Moses, which is further proof of my husband Alvin's claim that I am bossier than God.

5

Baked Cheesecakes

MOTHER WONDERFUL'S
BASIC LIME-ALMOND CHEESECAKE

Preheat oven to 350° F.
Ingredients need not be at room temperature.

Crust

10″ SPRINGFORM		8″ SPRINGFORM
1/4 pound (1 stick)	Lightly salted butter	4 tablespoons (1/2 stick)
2 cups	Finely ground vanilla wafer crumbs	1 cup + 2 tablespoons
1/4 cup	Sugar	2 tablespoons

Melt butter over very low heat. Combine butter with crumbs and sugar in a food processor until thoroughly blended (my preference) or stir and mash together with a fork in a roomy bowl. Wrap your fingers in plastic wrap, using the wrap like a protective mitten to keep fingers from getting greasy and to stop crust mix from sticking to them. First press small amounts of crumb mix all the way up the sides of an ungreased 10-inch springform (2 inches up the sides of an ungreased 8-inch springform); then sprinkle remaining crust mix over bottom of the springform. There should be enough crumb mix to cover the entire bottom if you haven't nibbled on it. If there are empty spots in the bottom, press the sides a little flatter and transfer the excess to the bottom, or just sprinkle a few more cookie crumbs in the blank spots to fill them in. Spread plastic wrap over the bottom and pat crust down firmly. Discard plastic wrap.

Filling

10″ SPRINGFORM		8″ SPRINGFORM
2 pounds (four 8-ounce packages)	Cream cheese	1 pound (two 8-ounce packages)
1 1/2 cups	Sugar	3/4 cup
1 1/2 tablespoons	Fresh lime juice	2 1/4 teaspoons
pinch	Salt	pinch
4	Large eggs	2

In a mixer, whip cream cheese on the highest speed for 5 minutes, then add sugar and whip for 2 minutes more. Add lime juice and salt and blend together thoroughly. Add the eggs, one at a time, keeping the mixer on the lowest speed in order to prevent too much air from destroying the proper consistency of the batter; mix just until each egg has been incorporated into the batter. Or:

If using a food processor, put the sugar in first. Cut each 8-ounce block of cream cheese into eight 1-inch cubes and add the first 8 cubes to bowl. Process, using on-off pulse, about 25 times, and then add the rest of the cream cheese cubes gradually, blending them in with on-off pulses until mixture is smooth and creamy. When you think it's perfect, blend nonstop for 20 seconds more, then blend in lime juice and salt for 5 seconds. Crack eggs in a bowl, break them up slightly with a fork, add them to batter in processor bowl, and fold them lightly into batter with a rubber spatula to prevent them from sinking to the bottom. Cut the eggs into the batter by using the on-off pulse 10 times, then scrape down the sides with a rubber spatula and pulse on-off 5 times more.

Pour batter into crust and bake in preheated oven.

Baking Time

10″ SPRINGFORM	8″ SPRINGFORM
55 minutes	40 minutes

Remove from oven and let stand on a counter for 10 minutes while you prepare the glaze. This 10-minute rest is a very essential step because it allows the interior of the cake to solidify without over-baking, burning, and/or cracking the exterior.

Sour Cream Glaze

10″ SPRINGFORM		8″ SPRINGFORM
2 cups	Sour cream	*1 cup*
¼ cup	Sugar	*2 tablespoons*
1 teaspoon	Almond extract	*½ teaspoon*

Combine sour cream, sugar, and extract with a rubber spatula in a plastic bowl. Spread evenly and smoothly over top of baked filling and return to 350° F oven for 10 minutes. Remove from oven and *immediately* place in refrigerator to cool, to prevent cracks from forming in the cake.

To remove cake from springform, let it stand at room temperature for 10 minutes to allow the butter to loosen its bond with the metal ring. When you release the springform clasp, the crust will detach naturally from the sides. If any small segments stick to the sides, loosen them by separating the crust from the sides gently with a metal spatula or a sharp knife.

MOTHER WONDERFUL'S
CHOCOLATE SWIRL CHEESECAKE

Preheat oven to 350° F.
Ingredients need not be at room temperature.

Crust

10" SPRINGFORM		8" SPRINGFORM
1/4 pound (1 stick)	Lightly salted butter	4 tablespoons (1/2 stick)
2 cups	Finely ground crisp chocolate cookie crumbs	1 cup + 2 tablespoons
1/4 cup	Sugar	2 tablespoons

Melt butter over very low heat. Combine butter with crumbs and sugar in a food processor or with a fork until thoroughly blended. Press small amounts of crumb mix all the way up the sides of an ungreased 10-inch springform (2 inches up the sides of an ungreased 8-inch springform) and then press remaining crust mix over bottom of springform. For a more detailed explanation of how to blend and lay down the crust, see pages 17-18.

Filling

10" SPRINGFORM		8" SPRINGFORM
2 ounces	Sweet chocolate	1 ounce
2 pounds (four 8-ounce packages)	Cream cheese	1 pound (two 8-ounce packages)
1 1/2 cups	Sugar	3/4 cup
1 tablespoon	Dark rum	1 1/2 teaspoons

10″ SPRINGFORM		8″ SPRINGFORM
1 1/2 *teaspoons*	Vanilla extract	3/4 *teaspoon*
pinch	Salt	*pinch*
4	Large eggs	2
1/4 *teaspoon*	Instant espresso	1/8 *teaspoon*

Melt sweet chocolate over simmering water in the top of a double boiler, in a frying pan over a heat-diffusing disk, or in a microwave oven, and reserve. (You can purchase a metal round with holes in it that conducts heat to the bottom of the pan indirectly so the pan really works just like a double boiler.)

In a mixer, whip cream cheese on the highest speed for 5 minutes, then add sugar and beat for 2 minutes more. Add rum, vanilla, and salt and blend together thoroughly. Add the eggs, one at a time, keeping the mixer on the *lowest speed* in order to prevent too much air from destroying the proper consistency of the batter; mix just until each egg has been incorporated into the batter. *Or:*

If using a food processor, put the sugar in first. Cut each 8-ounce block of cream cheese into eight 1-inch cubes and add the first 8 cubes to bowl. Process using on-off pulse about 25 times, and then add the rest of the cream cheese cubes gradually, blending them in with on-off pulses until mixture is smooth and creamy. When you think it's perfect, blend nonstop for 20 seconds more, then blend in rum, vanilla, and salt and process for 10 seconds more. Crack eggs in a bowl, break them up slightly with a fork, add them to batter in processor bowl, and fold them lightly into batter with a rubber spatula to prevent them from sinking to the bottom. Cut the eggs into the batter by using the on-off pulse 10 times, then scrape down the sides with a rubber spatula and pulse on-off 5 times more.

Remove 1 cup of batter (1/2 cup for 8-inch size) and reserve. Pour remainder into crust. Add melted chocolate and instant espresso to the reserved cup of batter and blend well with a rubber spatula. Pour reserved batter into the center of the filling in the springform and cut through with a knife to achieve a swirl effect, but with the majority of the chocolate batter remaining in the center. Save a bit of melted chocolate to dribble onto the glaze for decoration.

Pour batter into crust and bake in preheated oven.

Baking Time

10″ SPRINGFORM	8″ SPRINGFORM
1 hour + 10 minutes	45 minutes

Remove from oven and let stand on a counter for 10 minutes while you prepare the glaze.

Sour Cream Glaze

10″ SPRINGFORM		8″ SPRINGFORM
2 cups	Sour cream	*1 cup*
¼ cup	Sugar	*2 tablespoons*
1 teaspoon	Almond extract	*½ teaspoon*

Combine sour cream, sugar, and extract with a rubber spatula in a plastic bowl. Spread evenly and smoothly over top of baked filling, decorate with Jackson Pollack-like designs made with leftover melted chocolate, and return to 350° F oven for 10 minutes. Remove from oven and *immediately* place in refrigerator to cool. This prevents cracks from forming in the cake.

For an explanation of how to remove the cake from the springform, see page 19.

MOTHER WONDERFUL'S
TRIPLE CHOCOLATE CHEESECAKE

Preheat oven to 350° F.
Ingredients need not be at room temperature.

Crust

10″ SPRINGFORM		8″ SPRINGFORM
1/4 *pound (1 stick)*	Lightly salted butter	*4 tablespoons (1/2 stick)*
2 cups	Finely ground crisp chocolate cookie crumbs	*1 cup + 2 tablespoons*
1/4 *cup*	Sugar	*2 tablespoons*

Melt butter over very low heat. Combine butter with crumbs and sugar in a food processor or with a fork until thoroughly blended. Press small amounts of crumb mix all the way up the sides of an ungreased 10-inch springform (2 inches up the sides of an ungreased 8-inch springform) and then press remaining crumb mix over bottom of springform. For a more detailed explanation of how to blend and lay down the crust, see pages 17-18.

Filling

10″ SPRINGFORM		8″ SPRINGFORM
4 ounces	Sweet chocolate	2 ounces
2 pounds (four 8-ounce packages)	Cream cheese	1 pound (two 8-ounce packages)
1 1/4 cups	Sugar	1/2 cup + 2 tablespoons
1 tablespoon	Dark rum	1 1/2 teaspoons
1 teaspoon	Vanilla extract	3/4 teaspoon
pinch	Salt	pinch
4	Large eggs	2
1/4 cup	Sweet chocolate chopped into chip-sized bits or mini-chocolate chips	2 tablespoons

Melt sweet chocolate over simmering water in the top of a double boiler, in a pan over a heat diffuser, or in a microwave oven, and reserve.

In a mixer, whip cream cheese on the highest speed for 5 minutes, then add sugar and beat for 2 minutes more. Add rum, vanilla, melted chocolate, and salt and blend together thoroughly. Add the eggs, one at a time, keeping the mixer on the *lowest speed* in order to prevent too much air from destroying the proper consistency of the batter; mix just until each egg has been incorporated into the batter. Fold in chocolate bits. *Or:*

If using a food processor, put the sugar in first. Cut each 8-ounce block of cream cheese into eight 1-inch cubes and add the first 8 cubes to bowl. Process, using on-off pulse about 25 times, and then add the rest of the cream cheese cubes gradually, blending them in with on-off pulses until mixture is smooth and creamy. When you think it's perfect, blend nonstop for 20 seconds more, then blend in rum, vanilla, salt, and melted chocolate, and process for 10 seconds more. Crack eggs in a bowl, break them up slightly with a fork, add them to batter in processor bowl, and fold them lightly into batter with a rubber spatula to prevent them from sinking to the bottom. Cut the eggs into the batter by using the on-off pulse 10 times, then scrape down the sides with a rubber spatula and pulse on-off 5 times more. Fold in chocolate bits.

Pour batter into crust and bake in preheated oven.

Baking Time

10″ SPRINGFORM	8″ SPRINGFORM
50 minutes	40 minutes

Remove from oven and let stand on a counter for 10 minutes while you prepare the glaze.

Sour Cream Glaze

10″ SPRINGFORM		8″ SPRINGFORM
2 cups	Sour cream	*1 cup*
¼ cup	Sugar	*2 tablespoons*
1 teaspoon	Almond extract	*½ teaspoon*
as needed	Shaved chocolate	*as needed*

Combine sour cream, sugar, and extract with a rubber spatula in a plastic bowl. Spread evenly and smoothly over top of baked filling and return to 350° F oven for 10 minutes. Remove from oven and *immediately* place in refrigerator to cool. This prevents cracks from forming in the cake. Before serving, sprinkle glaze with shaved or grated chocolate.

For an explanation of how to remove the cake from the springform, see page 19.

MOTHER WONDERFUL'S CHOCOLATE MINT CHEESECAKE

Preheat oven to 350° F.
Ingredients need not be at room temperature.

Crust

10″ SPRINGFORM		8″ SPRINGFORM
¼ pound (1 stick)	Lightly salted butter	*4 tablespoons (½ stick)*
2 cups	Finely ground crisp chocolate cookie crumbs	*1 cup + 2 tablespoons*
¼ cup	Sugar	*2 tablespoons*

Melt butter over very low heat. Combine butter with crumbs and sugar in a food processor or with a fork until thoroughly blended. Press small amounts of crumb mix all the way up the sides of an ungreased 10-inch springform (2 inches up the sides of an ungreased 8-inch springform) and then press remaining crumb mix over bottom of springform. For a more detailed explanation of how to blend and lay down the crust, see pages 17-18.

Filling

10″ SPRINGFORM		8″ SPRINGFORM
4 ounces	Sweet chocolate	*2 ounces*
2 ounces	Green chocolate mint soufflé (my preference) or mint-flavored chips	*1 ounce*
2 pounds (four 8-ounce packages)	Cream cheese	*1 pound (two 8-ounce packages)*
1 ¼ cups	Sugar	*½ cup + 2 tablespoons*
1 tablespoon	Vandermint liqueur	*1 ½ teaspoons*
1 teaspoon	Mint extract	*½ teaspoon*
pinch	Salt	*pinch*
4	Large eggs	*2*

Melt sweet chocolate over simmering water in the top of a double boiler, in a pan over a heat diffuser, or in a microwave oven, and reserve. Chop mint soufflé into small chips and reserve.

In a mixer, whip cream cheese on the highest speed for 5 minutes, then add sugar and whip for 2 minutes more. Add liqueur, extract, melted chocolate, mint-flavored chips, and salt and blend together thoroughly. Add the eggs, one at a time, keeping the mixer on the *lowest speed* in order to prevent too much air from destroying the proper consistency of the batter; mix just until each egg has been incorporated into the batter. *Or:*

If using a food processor, put the sugar in first. Cut each 8-ounce block of cream cheese into eight 1-inch cubes and add the first 8 cubes to bowl. Process, using on-off pulse about 25 times, and then add the rest of the cream cheese cubes gradually, blending them in with on-off pulses until mixture is smooth and creamy. When you think it's perfect, blend nonstop for 20 seconds more, then blend in liqueur, extract, melted chocolate, and salt and process for 10 seconds more. Crack eggs in a bowl, break them up slightly with a fork, add them to batter in processor bowl and fold them lightly into batter with a rubber spatula to prevent them from sinking to the bottom. Cut the eggs into the batter by using the on-off pulse 10 times, then scrape down the sides with a rubber spatula and pulse on-off 5 times more. Fold in mint-flavored bits with a rubber spatula.

Pour batter into crust and bake in preheated oven.

Baking Time

10″ SPRINGFORM	8″ SPRINGFORM
50 minutes	40 minutes

Remove from oven and let stand on a counter for 10 minutes while you prepare the glaze.

Sour Cream Glaze

10″ SPRINGFORM		8″ SPRINGFORM
2 cups	Sour cream	1 cup
1/4 cup	Sugar	2 tablespoons
1 teaspoon	White crème de menthe	1/2 teaspoon
as needed	Shaved chocolate soufflé	as needed

Combine sour cream, sugar, and crème de menthe with a rubber spatula in a plastic bowl. Spread evenly and smoothly over top of baked filling and return to 350° F oven for 10 minutes. Remove from oven and *immediately* place in refrigerator to cool. This prevents cracks from forming in the cake. Before serving, sprinkle top with shaved or grated chocolate soufflé.

For an explanation of how to remove the cake from the spring-form, see page 19.

MOTHER WONDERFUL'S
CHOCOLATE FOUR CHEESECAKE

Preheat oven to 350° F.
Ingredients need not be at room temperature.

Crust

10″ SPRINGFORM		8″ SPRINGFORM
1/4 pound (1 stick)	Lightly salted butter	4 tablespoons (1/2 stick)
1 cup	Finely ground crisp chocolate cookie crumbs	1/2 cup + 1 tablespoon
1 cup	Finely ground vanilla wafer crumbs	1/2 cup + 1 tablespoon
1/4 cup	Sugar	2 tablespoons

Melt butter over very low heat. Combine butter with crumbs and sugar in a food processor or with a fork until thoroughly blended. Press small amounts of crumb mix all the way up the sides of an ungreased 10-inch springform (2 inches up the sides of an ungreased 8-inch springform) and then press remaining crumb mix over bottom of springform. For a more detailed explanation of how to blend and lay down the crust, see pages 17-18.

Filling

10″ SPRINGFORM		8″ SPRINGFORM
1 ounce	Sweet dark chocolate	½ ounce
3 ounces	White chocolate	1½ ounces
2 pounds (four 8-ounce packages)	Cream cheese	1 pound (two 8-ounce packages)
1¼ cups	Sugar	½ cup + 2 tablespoons
1 tablespoon	Grand Marnier	1½ teaspoons
1½ teaspoons	Orange extract	¾ teaspoon
pinch	Salt	pinch
4	Large eggs	2
1 ounce	Orange-flavored chocolate bar, grated or chopped	½ ounce

Melt sweet dark chocolate over simmering water in the top of a double boiler, in a pan over a heat diffuser, or in a microwave oven, and reserve. Melt white chocolate separately and reserve.

In a mixer, whip cream cheese on the highest speed for 5 minutes, then add sugar and whip for 2 minutes more. Add Grand Marnier, orange extract, and salt and blend together thoroughly. Add the eggs, one at a time, keeping the mixer on the *lowest speed* in order to prevent too much air from destroying the proper consistency of the batter; mix just until each egg has been incorporated into the batter. *Or:*

If using a food processor, put the sugar in first. Cut each 8-ounce block of cream cheese into eight 1-inch cubes and add the first 8 cubes to bowl. Process, using on-off pulse about 25 times, and then add the rest of the cream cheese cubes gradually, blending them in with on-off pulses until mixture is smooth and creamy. When you think it's perfect, blend nonstop for 20 seconds more, then blend in Grand Marnier, orange extract, and salt and process for 10 seconds more. Crack eggs in a bowl, break them up slightly with a fork, add them to batter in processor bowl, and fold them lightly into batter with a rubber spatula to prevent them from sinking to the bottom. Cut the eggs into the batter by using the on-off pulse 10 times, then scrape down the sides with a rubber spatula.

Reserve 1 cup batter (½ cup for 8-inch cake). Add melted white chocolate and grated orange-flavored chocolate to remaining batter and fold in on lowest speed of mixer if you are using a mixer or blend in with 5 on-off pulses if you are using a food processor. Pour batter into crust. Fold melted sweet chocolate into reserved batter and blend thoroughly with a rubber spatula. Pour chocolate batter into center of the batter in the pan and cut through with a knife to achieve a swirl effect, but most of the sweet chocolate mixture should remain in the center of the cake. Save a bit of melted dark chocolate for decorating the glaze.

Pour batter into crust and bake in preheated oven.

Baking Time

10″ SPRINGFORM	8″ SPRINGFORM
50 minutes	40 minutes

Remove from oven and let stand on a counter for 10 minutes while you prepare the glaze.

Sour Cream Glaze

10″ SPRINGFORM		8″ SPRINGFORM
2 cups	Sour cream	1 cup
¼ cup	Sugar	2 tablespoons
1 teaspoon	Grand Marnier	½ teaspoon

Combine sour cream, sugar, and Grand Marnier with a rubber spatula in a plastic bowl. Spread evenly and smoothly over top of baked filling, make decorative swirls on the glaze with any leftover melted sweet chocolate, and return to 350° F oven for 10 minutes. Remove from oven and *immediately* place in refrigerator to cool. This prevents cracks from forming in the cake.

For an explanation of how to remove the cake from the springform, see page 19.

NEW FLAVOR!

MOTHER WONDERFUL'S
CHOCOLATE RASPBERRY CHEESECAKE

Preheat oven to 350° F.
Ingredients need not be at room temperature.

Crust

10″ SPRINGFORM		8″ SPRINGFORM
¼ pound (1 stick)	Lightly salted butter	*4 tablespoons (½ stick)*
2 cups	Finely ground crisp chocolate cookie crumbs	*1 cup + 2 tablespoons*
¼ cup	Sugar	*2 tablespoons*

Melt butter over very low heat. Combine butter with crumbs and sugar in a food processor or with a fork until thoroughly blended. Press small amounts of crumb mix all the way up the sides of an ungreased 10-inch springform (2 inches up the sides of an ungreased 8-inch springform) and then press remaining crumb mix over bottom of springform. For a more detailed explanation of how to blend and lay down the crust, see pages 17-18.

Filling

10″ SPRINGFORM		8″ SPRINGFORM
2 ounces	Sweet chocolate	*1 ounce*
2 pounds (four 8-ounce packages)	Cream cheese	*1 pound (two 8-ounce packages)*
1 ½ cups	Sugar	*³/₄ cup*
1 tablespoon	Raspberry extract	*1 ½ teaspoons*
1 ½ teaspoons	Chocolate extract	*³/₄ teaspoon*
pinch	Salt	*pinch*
4	Large eggs	*2*
1 cup	Fresh raspberries	*¹/₂ cup*

Melt sweet chocolate over simmering water in the top of a double boiler, in a pan over a heat diffuser, or in a microwave oven, and reserve.

In a mixer, whip cream cheese on the highest speed for 5 minutes, then add sugar and whip for 2 minutes or more. Add melted chocolate, extracts, and salt and blend together thoroughly. Add the eggs, one at a time, keeping the mixer on the *lowest speed* in order to prevent too much air from destroying the proper consistency of the batter; mix just until each egg has been incorporated into the batter. Fold in raspberries with a rubber spatula. *Or:*

If using a food processor, put the sugar in first. Cut each 8-ounce block of cream cheese into eight 1-inch cubes and add the first 8 cubes to bowl. Process using on-off pulse about 25 times, and then add the rest of the cream cheese cubes gradually, blending them in with on-off pulses until mixture is smooth and creamy. When you think it's perfect, blend nonstop for 20 seconds more, then blend in melted chocolate, extracts, and salt for 10 seconds. Crack eggs in a bowl, break them up slightly with a fork, add them to batter in processor bowl, and fold them lightly into batter with a rubber spatula to prevent them from sinking to the bottom. Cut the eggs into the batter by using the on-off pulse 10 times, then scrape down the sides with a rubber spatula, and pulse on-off 5 times more. Fold in raspberries with a rubber spatula.

Pour batter into crust and bake in preheated oven.

Baking Time

10″ SPRINGFORM	8″ SPRINGFORM
55 minutes	40 minutes

Remove from oven and let stand on a counter for 10 minutes while you prepare the glaze.

Sour Cream Glaze

10″ SPRINGFORM		8″ SPRINGFORM
2 cups	Sour cream	1 cup
1/4 cup	Sugar	2 tablespoons
1 teaspoon	Raspberry liqueur	1/2 teaspoon
as required	Shaved sweet chocolate	as required
as required	Fresh raspberries	as required

Combine sour cream, sugar, and liqueur with a rubber spatula in a plastic bowl. Spread evenly and smoothly over top of baked filling and return to 350° F oven for 10 minutes. Remove from oven and *immediately* place in refrigerator to cool to prevent cracks from forming in the cake. Before serving, sprinkle with shaved sweet chocolate and some fresh raspberries.

For an explanation of how to remove the cake from the springform, see page 19.

MOTHER WONDERFUL'S
WHITE CHOCOLATE CASSIS CHEESECAKE

Preheat oven to 350° F.
Ingredients need not be at room temperature.

Crust

10″ SPRINGFORM		8″ SPRINGFORM
¼ pound (1 stick)	Lightly salted butter	4 tablespoons (½ stick)
1 ounce	Grated white chocolate	½ ounce
2 cups	Finely ground arrowroot tea biscuit crumbs	1 cup + 2 tablespoons
¼ cup	Sugar	2 tablespoons

Melt butter over very low heat. Combine butter with white chocolate, crumbs, and sugar in a food processor or with a fork until thoroughly blended. Press small amounts of crumb mix all the way up the sides of an ungreased 10-inch springform (2 inches up the sides of an ungreased 8-inch springform) and then press remaining crumb mix over bottom of springform. For a more detailed explanation of how to blend and lay down the crust, see pages 17-18.

Filling

10″ SPRINGFORM		8″ SPRINGFORM
2 pounds (four 8-ounce packages)	Cream cheese	1 pound (two 8-ounce packages)
1¼ cups	Sugar	½ cup + 2 tablespoons
4 ounces	White chocolate	2 ounces
3 tablespoons	Cassis	1½ tablespoons
pinch	Salt	pinch
4	Large eggs	2

In a mixer, whip cream cheese on the highest speed for 5 minutes, then add sugar and beat for 2 minutes more. Shave or slice white chocolate very thin, then add to batter with cassis and salt and blend together thoroughly. Add the eggs, one at a time, keeping the mixer on the *lowest speed* in order to prevent too much air from destroying the proper consistency of the batter; mix just until each egg has been incorporated into the batter. *Or:*

If using a food processor, put the sugar in first. Cut each 8-ounce block of cream cheese into eight 1-inch cubes and add the first 8 cubes to bowl. Process using on-off pulse about 25 times, and then add the rest of the cream cheese cubes gradually, blending them in with on-off pulses until mixture is smooth and creamy. When you think it's perfect, blend nonstop for 20 seconds more, then blend in cassis and salt for 5 seconds. Crack eggs in a bowl, break them up slightly with a fork, add them to batter in processor bowl, and fold them lightly into batter with a rubber spatula to prevent them from sinking to the bottom. Cut the eggs into the batter by using the on-off pulse 10 times, then scrape down the sides with a rubber spatula and pulse on-off 5 times more. Slice or shave white chocolate very thin and fold into batter with a rubber spatula.

Pour batter into crust and bake in preheated oven.

Baking Time

10″ SPRINGFORM	8″ SPRINGFORM
50 minutes	40 minutes

Remove from oven and let stand on a counter for 10 minutes while you prepare the glaze.

Sour Cream Glaze

10″ SPRINGFORM		8″ SPRINGFORM
2 *cups*	Sour cream	1 *cup*
¼ *cup*	Sugar	2 *tablespoons*
1 *teaspoon*	Almond extract	½ *teaspoon*
as needed	White chocolate	*as needed*

Combine sour cream, sugar, and extract with a rubber spatula in a plastic bowl. Spread evenly and smoothly over top of baked filling and return to 350° F oven for 10 minutes. Remove from oven and *immediately* place in refrigerator to cool to prevent cracks from forming in the cake. Shave white chocolate very thin and decorate top of cake with it before serving.

For an explanation of how to remove the cake from the springform, see page 19.

MOTHER WONDERFUL'S
ALMOND JOY CHEESECAKE

Preheat oven to 350° F.
Ingredients need not be at room temperature.

Crust

10″ SPRINGFORM		8″ SPRINGFORM
¼ pound (1 stick)	Lightly salted butter	4 tablespoons (½ stick)
2 cups	Finely ground crisp chocolate cookie crumbs	1 cup + 2 tablespoons
¼ cup	Sugar	2 tablespoons

Melt butter over very low heat. Combine butter with crumbs and sugar in a food processor or with a fork until thoroughly blended. Press small amounts of crumb mix all the way up the sides of an ungreased 10-inch springform (2 inches up the sides of an ungreased 8-inch springform) and then press remaining crumb mix over bottom of springform. For a more detailed explanation of how to blend and lay down the crust, see pages 17-18.

Filling

10″ SPRINGFORM		8″ SPRINGFORM
2 pounds (four 8-ounce packages)	Cream cheese	1 pound (two 8-ounce packages)
1½ cups	Sugar	¾ cup
1 teaspoon	Amaretto extract	½ teaspoon
1 teaspoon	Almond extract	½ teaspoon

10″ SPRINGFORM		8″ SPRINGFORM
½ cup	Coarsely chopped almonds with skins	*¼ cup*
pinch	Salt	*pinch*
4	Large eggs	*2*

In a mixer, whip cream cheese on the highest speed for 5 minutes, then add sugar and beat for 2 minutes more. Add extracts, almonds, and salt and blend together thoroughly. Add the eggs, one at a time, keeping the mixer on the *lowest speed* in order to prevent too much air from destroying the proper consistency of the batter; mix just until each egg has been incorporated into the batter. *Or:*

If using a food processor, put the sugar in first. Cut each 8-ounce block of cream cheese into eight 1-inch cubes and add the first 8 cubes to bowl. Process using on-off pulse about 25 times, and then add the rest of the cream cheese cubes gradually, blending them in with on-off pulses until mixture is smooth and creamy. When you think it's perfect, blend nonstop for 20 seconds more, then blend in extracts, almonds, and salt and process for 10 seconds more. Crack eggs in a bowl, break them up slightly with a fork, add them to batter in processor bowl, and fold them lightly into batter with a rubber spatula to prevent them from sinking to the bottom. Cut the eggs into the batter by using the on-off pulse 10 times, then scrape down the sides with a rubber spatula and pulse on-off 5 times more.

Pour batter into crust and bake in preheated oven.

Baking Time

10″ SPRINGFORM	8″ SPRINGFORM
50 minutes	40 minutes

Remove from oven and let stand on a counter for 10 minutes while you prepare the glaze.

Sour Cream Glaze

10″ SPRINGFORM		8″ SPRINGFORM
2 cups	Sour cream	1 cup
¼ cup	Sugar	2 tablespoons
1 teaspoon	Coconut extract	½ teaspoon
½ cup	Grated coconut	¼ cup
¼ cup	Blanched, sliced almonds	2 tablespoons

Combine sour cream, sugar, and extract with a rubber spatula in a plastic bowl. Spread evenly and smoothly over top of baked filling, sprinkle first with coconut and then with almonds, and return to 350° F oven for 10 minutes. Remove from oven and *immediately* place in refrigerator to cool. This prevents cracks from forming in the cake.

For an explanation of how to remove the cake from the spring-form, see page 19.

MOTHER WONDERFUL'S
APRICOT ALMOND CHEESECAKE

Preheat oven to 350° F.
Ingredients need not be at room temperature.

Crust

10″ SPRINGFORM		8″ SPRINGFORM
¼ pound (1 stick)	Lightly salted butter	4 tablespoons (½ stick)
2 cups	Finely ground vanilla wafer crumbs	1 cup + 2 tablespoons
¼ cup	Sugar	2 tablespoons

Melt butter over very low heat. Combine butter with crumbs and sugar in a food processor or with a fork until thoroughly blended. Press small amounts of crumb mix all the way up the sides of an ungreased 10-inch springform (2 inches up the sides of an ungreased 8-inch springform) and then press remaining crumb mix over bottom of springform. For a more detailed explanation of how to blend and lay down the crust, see pages 17-18.

Filling

10" SPRINGFORM		8" SPRINGFORM
2 pounds (four 8-ounce packages)	Cream cheese	1 pound (two 8-ounce packages)
1½ cups	Sugar	¾ cup
½ teaspoon	Almond extract	¼ teaspoon
1 teaspoon	Orange extract	½ teaspoon
1 tablespoon	Grand Marnier	1½ teaspoons
pinch	Salt	pinch
4	Large eggs	2
½ cup	Sliced almonds with skin	¼ cup
4	Honey-glazed apricot halves*	2

*Honey-glazed apricots are available in any store that sells nuts and dried fruits. The apricots are dried first and then dipped in honey. They are sticky and sweet, not as hard as regular dried apricots. But if you can't find them, use regular dried apricots.

In a mixer, whip cream cheese on the highest speed for 5 minutes, then add sugar and whip for 2 minutes more. Add extracts, Grand Marnier, and salt and blend thoroughly. Add the eggs, one at a time, keeping the mixer on the *lowest speed* in order to prevent too much air from destroying the proper consistency of the batter; mix just until each egg has been incorporated into the batter. *Or:*

If using a food processor, put the sugar in first. Cut each 8-ounce block of cream cheese into eight 1-inch cubes and add the first 8 cubes to bowl. Process using on-off pulse about 25 times, and then add the rest of the cream cheese cubes gradually, blending them in with on-off pulses until mixture is smooth and creamy. When you think it's perfect, blend nonstop for 20 seconds more, then blend in extracts, Grand Marnier, and salt for 5 seconds. Crack eggs in a bowl, break them up slightly with a fork, add them to batter in processor bowl, and fold them lightly into batter with a rubber spatula to prevent them from sinking to the bottom. Cut the eggs into the batter by using the on-off pulse 10 times, then scrape down the sides with a rubber spatula and pulse on-off 5 times more.

Slice apricot halves thin. Pour ⅓ of the batter into crust. Sprinkle with ½ of the almonds. Top with another ⅓ of the batter. Insert apricot slices vertically into batter and sprinkle with remaining almonds. Top with remaining batter and bake in preheated oven.

Baking Time

10″ SPRINGFORM	8″ SPRINGFORM
50 minutes	40 minutes

Remove from oven and let stand on a counter for 10 minutes while you prepare the glaze.

Sour Cream Glaze

10″ SPRINGFORM		8″ SPRINGFORM
2 cups	Sour cream	1 cup
¼ cup	Sugar	2 tablespoons
1 teaspoon	Almond extract	½ teaspoon
2	Honey-glazed apricot halves	2
¼ cup	Sliced almonds with skin	2 tablespoons

Combine sour cream, sugar, and extract with a rubber spatula in a plastic bowl. Spread evenly and smoothly over top of baked filling. Cut apricot into 12 slices and arrange slices vertically around the edge like the numbers on a clock face. Sprinkle with almonds. Return to 350° F oven for 10 minutes. Remove from oven and *immediately* place in refrigerator to cool to prevent cracks from forming in the cake.

For an explanation of how to remove the cake from the spring-form, see page 19.

MOTHER WONDERFUL'S
APRICOT STREUSEL CHEESECAKE

Preheat oven to 350° F.
Ingredients need not be at room temperature.

Preliminary

10″ SPRINGFORM		8″ SPRINGFORM
¼ cup	Sugar	2 tablespoons
¼ cup	Chopped walnuts	2 tablespoons
½ teaspoon	Cinnamon	¼ teaspoon

Combine ingredients in bowl and set aside. Reserve 2 tablespoons to sprinkle on glaze. The rest will be layered into the cheesecake.

Crust

10″ SPRINGFORM		8″ SPRINGFORM
¼ pound (1 stick)	Lightly salted butter	4 tablespoons (½ stick)
2 cups	Finely ground cinnamon-flavored graham cracker crumbs	1 cup + 2 tablespoons
¼ cup	Sugar	2 tablespoons

Melt butter over very low heat. Combine butter with crumbs and sugar in a food processor or with a fork until thoroughly blended. Press small amounts of crumb mix all the way up the sides of an ungreased 10-inch springform (2 inches up the sides of an ungreased 8-inch springform) and then press remaining crumb mix over bottom of springform. For a more detailed explanation of how to blend and lay down the crust, see pages 17-18.

Filling

10″ SPRINGFORM		8″ SPRINGFORM
2 pounds (four 8-ounce packages)	Cream cheese	1 pound (two 8-ounce packages)
1 cup	Sugar	1/2 cup
1 1/2 tablespoons	Vanilla extract	2 1/4 teaspoons
1/4 teaspoon	Apricot brandy or apricot brandy extract	1/8 teaspoon
1 tablespoon	Dark rum	1 1/2 teaspoons
pinch	Salt	pinch
4	Large eggs	2
1/2 cup	Apricot preserves	1/4 cup
2 tablespoons	Cinnamon-nut mixture previously prepared	1 tablespoon

In a mixer, whip cream cheese on the highest speed for 5 minutes, then add sugar and beat for 2 minutes more. Add extracts, rum, and salt and blend thoroughly. Add the eggs, one at a time, keeping the mixer on the *lowest speed* in order to prevent too much air from destroying the proper consistency of the batter; mix just until each egg has been incorporated into the batter. *Or:*

If using a food processor, put the sugar in first. Cut each 8-ounce block of cream cheese into eight 1-inch cubes and add the first 8 cubes to bowl. Process using on-off pulse about 25 times, and then add the rest of the cream cheese cubes gradually, blending them in with on-off pulses until mixture is smooth and creamy. When you think it's perfect, blend nonstop for 20 seconds more, then blend in extracts, rum, and salt for 5 seconds. Crack eggs in a bowl, break them up slightly with a fork, add them to batter in processor bowl, and fold them lightly into batter with a rubber spatula to prevent them from sinking to the bottom. Cut the eggs into the batter by using the on-off pulse 10 times, then scrape down the sides with a rubber spatula and pulse on-off 5 times more.

Remove 1 cup (½ cup for 8-inch cake) of batter and with a rubber spatula blend in preserves and reserve. Pour ½ of the nonreserved batter into the crust. Sprinkle with half of the cinnamon-nut mixture and spread a second layer of batter over the nuts. Sprinkle with remaining nut mixture and cover with reserved batter-preserves mixture. Cut through with a knife to achieve a swirl effect.

Bake in preheated oven.

Baking Time

10″ SPRINGFORM	8″ SPRINGFORM
1 hour + 10 minutes	50 minutes

Remove from oven and let stand on a counter for 10 minutes while you prepare the glaze.

Sour Cream Glaze

10″ SPRINGFORM		8″ SPRINGFORM
2 cups	Sour cream	1 cup
¼ cup	Sugar	2 tablespoons
½ teaspoon	Vanilla extract	¼ teaspoon
½ teaspoon	Dark rum	¼ teaspoon
2 tablespoons	Cinnamon-nut mixture	2 tablespoons

Combine sour cream, sugar, extract, and rum with a rubber spatula in a plastic bowl. Spread evenly and smoothly over top of baked filling. Sprinkle with cinnamon-nut mixture and return to 350° F oven for 10 minutes. Remove from oven and *immediately* place in refrigerator to cool to prevent cracks from forming in the cake.

For an explanation of how to remove the cake from the spring-form, see page 19.

MOTHER WONDERFUL'S
PIÑA COLADA CHEESECAKE

Preliminary

10″ SPRINGFORM		8″ SPRINGFORM
2 *round slices*	Dried pineapple	1 *round slice*
3 *tablespoons*	Dark rum	1 ½ *tablespoons*

Cut pineapple into thin slices and soak in rum. When ready to make filling, drain pineapple, and reserve rum and pineapple separately.

Preheat oven to 350° F.
Ingredients need not be at room temperature.

Crust

10″ SPRINGFORM		8″ SPRINGFORM
¼ *pound (1 stick)*	Lightly salted butter	4 *tablespoons* (½ *stick*)
2 *cups*	Finely ground vanilla wafer crumbs	1 *cup* + 2 *tablespoons*
¼ *cup*	Sugar	2 *tablespoons*

Melt butter over very low heat. Combine butter with crumbs and sugar in a food processor or with a fork until thoroughly blended. Press small amounts of crumb mix all the way up the sides of an ungreased 10-inch springform (2 inches up the sides of an ungreased 8-inch springform) and then press remaining crumb mix over bottom of springform. For a more detailed explanation of how to blend and lay down the crust, see pages 17-18.

Filling

10″ SPRINGFORM		8″ SPRINGFORM
2 pounds (four 8-ounce packages)	Cream cheese	1 pound (two 8-ounce packages)
1 1/2 cups	Sugar	3/4 cup
2 teaspoons	Pineapple extract	1 teaspoon
1 tablespoon	Dark rum in which pineapple was soaked	1 1/2 teaspoons
2 slices	Drained, rum-soaked sliced pineapple	1 slice
pinch	Salt	pinch
4	Large eggs	2

In a mixer, whip cream cheese on the highest speed for 5 minutes, then add sugar and beat for 2 minutes more. Add extract, rum, pineapple, and salt and blend thoroughly. Add the eggs, one at a time, keeping the mixer on the lowest speed in order to prevent too much air from destroying the proper consistency of the batter; mix just until each egg has been incorporated into the batter. Or:

If using a food processor, put the sugar in first. Cut each 8-ounce block of cream cheese into eight 1-inch cubes and add the first 8 cubes to bowl. Process using on-off pulse about 25 times, and then add the rest of the cream cheese cubes gradually, blending them in with on-off pulses until mixture is smooth and creamy. When you think it's perfect, blend nonstop for 20 seconds more, then blend in extract, rum, and salt for 5 seconds. Crack eggs in a bowl, break them up slightly with a fork, add them to batter in processor bowl, and fold them lightly into batter with a rubber spatula to prevent them from sinking to the bottom. Cut the eggs into the batter by using the on-off pulse 10 times, then scrape down the sides with a rubber spatula and pulse on-off 5 times more. Fold drained sliced pineapple into batter with a rubber spatula.

Pour batter into crust and bake in preheated oven.

Baking Time

10″ SPRINGFORM	8″ SPRINGFORM
55 minutes	40 minutes

Remove from oven and let stand on a counter for 10 minutes while you prepare the glaze.

Sour Cream Glaze

10″ SPRINGFORM		8″ SPRINGFORM
2 cups	Sour cream	1 cup
1/4 cup	Sugar	2 tablespoons
1 teaspoon	Coconut extract	1/2 teaspoon
1/2 cup	Grated coconut	1/4 cup

Combine sour cream, sugar, and coconut extract with a rubber spatula in a plastic bowl. Spread evenly and smoothly over top of baked filling and sprinkle coconut over top. Return to 350° F oven for 10 minutes. Remove from oven and *immediately* place in refrigerator to cool to prevent cracks from forming in the cake.

For an explanation of how to remove the cake from the springform, see page 19.

MOTHER WONDERFUL'S
BANANA DAIQUIRI CHEESECAKE

Preheat oven to 350° F.
Ingredients need not be at room temperature.

Crust

10" SPRINGFORM		8" SPRINGFORM
1/4 pound (1 stick)	Lightly salted butter	4 tablespoons (1/2 stick)
2 cups	Finely ground vanilla wafer crumbs	1 cup + 2 tablespoons
1/4 cup	Sugar	2 tablespoons

Melt butter over very low heat. Combine butter with crumbs and sugar in a food processor or with a fork until thoroughly blended. Press small amounts of crumb mix all the way up the sides of an ungreased 10-inch springform (2 inches up the sides of an ungreased 8-inch springform) and then press remaining crumb mix over bottom of springform. For a more detailed explanation of how to blend and lay down the crust, see pages 17-18.

Filling

10" SPRINGFORM		8" SPRINGFORM
2 pounds (four 8-ounce packages)	Cream cheese	1 pound (two 8-ounce packages)
1 1/2 cups	Sugar	3/4 cup
5 teaspoons	Banana extract	2 1/2 teaspoons
1 teaspoon	Dark rum	1/2 teaspoon

10″ SPRINGFORM		8″ SPRINGFORM
1 *teaspoon*	Fresh lime juice	¹/₂ *teaspoon*
¹/₂	Ripe, mushy banana mashed with a fork	¹/₄
pinch	Salt	*pinch*
4	Large eggs	2
1 ¹/₂	Ripe bananas, thinly sliced	³/₄

In a mixer, whip cream cheese on the highest speed for 5 minutes, then add sugar and beat for 2 minutes more. Add extract, rum, lime juice, mashed banana, and salt and blend thoroughly. Add the eggs, one at a time, keeping the mixer on the *lowest speed* in order to prevent too much air from destroying the proper consistency of the batter; mix just until each egg has been incorporated into the batter. *Or:*

If using a food processor, put the sugar in first. Cut each 8-ounce block of cream cheese into eight 1-inch cubes and add the first 8 cubes to bowl. Process using on-off pulse about 25 times, and then add the rest of the cream cheese cubes gradually, blending them in with on-off pulses until mixture is smooth and creamy. When you think it's perfect, blend nonstop for 20 seconds more, then blend in extract, rum, lime juice, mashed banana, and salt for 5 seconds. Crack eggs in a bowl, break them up slightly with a fork, add them to batter in processor bowl, and fold them lightly into batter with a rubber spatula to prevent them from sinking to the bottom. Cut the eggs into the batter by using the on-off pulse 10 times, then scrape down the sides with a rubber spatula and pulse on-off 5 times more.

Pour half of the batter into the crust. Insert banana slices vertically into the batter. Pour remaining batter on top and bake in preheated oven.

Baking Time

10″ SPRINGFORM	8″ SPRINGFORM
55 minutes	40 minutes

Remove from oven and let stand on a counter for 10 minutes while you prepare the glaze.

Sour Cream Glaze

10″ SPRINGFORM		8″ SPRINGFORM
2 cups	Sour cream	1 cup
¼ cup	Sugar	2 tablespoons
1 teaspoon	Coconut extract	½ teaspoon
½ cup	Grated coconut	¼ cup

Combine sour cream, sugar, and coconut extract with a rubber spatula in a plastic bowl. Spread evenly and smoothly over top of baked filling and sprinkle coconut over top. Return to 350° F oven for 10 minutes. Remove from oven and *immediately* place in refrigerator to cool to prevent cracks from forming in the cake.

For an explanation of how to remove the cake from the springform, see page 19.

MOTHER WONDERFUL'S
GINGER PEAR CHEESECAKE

Preliminary

10″ SPRINGFORM		8″ SPRINGFORM
2	Dried pear halves	1
3 tablespoons	Fine cognac	1 ½ tablespoons

Cut pears into slivers and soak in cognac. When ready to make filling, drain and reserve pears and cognac separately.

Preheat oven to 350 degrees F.
Ingredients need not be at room temperature.

Crust

10″ SPRINGFORM		8″ SPRINGFORM
¼ pound (1 stick)	Lightly salted butter	4 tablespoons (½ stick)
1 cup	Finely ground gingersnap crumbs	½ cup + 1 tablespoon
1 cup	Finely ground vanilla wafer crumbs	½ cup + 1 tablespoon
¼ cup	Sugar	2 tablespoons

Melt butter over very low heat. Combine butter with crumbs and sugar in a food processor or with a fork until thoroughly blended. Press small amounts of crumb mix all the way up the sides of an ungreased 10-inch springform (2 inches up the sides of an ungreased

8-inch springform) and then press remaining crust mix over bottom of springform. For a more detailed explanation of how to blend and lay down the crust, see pages 17-18.

Filling

10″ SPRINGFORM		8″ SPRINGFORM
2 pounds (four 8-ounce packages)	Cream cheese	1 pound (two 8-ounce packages)
1½ cups	Sugar	¾ cup
1½ tablespoons	Reserved cognac	2¼ teaspoons
½ teaspoon	Vanilla extract	¼ teaspoon
pinch	Salt	pinch
4	Large eggs	2
	Reserved slivered, cognac-soaked pears	
2 chunks	Crystallized ginger	1 chunk

In a mixer, whip cream cheese on the highest speed for 5 minutes, then add sugar and beat for 2 minutes more. Add reserved cognac, vanilla, and salt and blend together thoroughly. Add the eggs, one at a time, keeping the mixer on the *lowest speed* in order to prevent too much air from destroying the proper consistency of the batter; mix just until each egg has been incorporated into the batter. Slice ginger very thin and fold ginger and slivered pears into batter with a rubber spatula. *Or:*

If using a food processor, put the sugar in first. Cut each 8-ounce block of cream cheese into eight 1-inch cubes and add the first 8 cubes to bowl. Process using on-off pulse about 25 times, and then add the rest of the cream cheese cubes gradually, blending them in with on-off pulses until mixture is smooth and creamy. When you think it's perfect, blend nonstop for 20 seconds more, then blend in 1½ tablespoons reserved cognac, vanilla, and salt for 5 seconds. Crack eggs in a bowl, break them up slightly with a fork, add them to batter in processor bowl, and fold them lightly into batter with a rubber spatula to prevent them from sinking to the bottom. Cut the eggs into the batter by using the on-off pulse 10 times, then scrape down the sides with a rubber spatula and pulse on-off 5 times more. Fold in pears and ginger with a rubber spatula.

Pour batter into crust and bake in preheated oven.

Baking Time

10″ SPRINGFORM	8″ SPRINGFORM
55 minutes	40 minutes

Remove from oven and let stand on a counter for 10 minutes while you prepare the glaze.

Sour Cream Glaze

10″ SPRINGFORM		8″ SPRINGFORM
2 cups	Sour cream	1 cup
1/4 cup	Sugar	2 tablespoons
1/2 teaspoon	Reserved cognac	1/4 teaspoon
1/2 teaspoon	Vanilla extract	1/4 teaspoon
4 drops	Ginger extract	2 drops
1 chunk	Crystallized ginger	1 chunk

Combine sour cream, sugar, cognac, and extracts with a rubber spatula in a plastic bowl. Spread evenly and smoothly over top of baked filling. Slice ginger into 12 slivers and arrange ginger slices vertically around the rim of the glaze like numbers on a clock face. Return cake to 350° F oven for 10 minutes. Remove from oven and *immediately* place in refrigerator to cool to prevent cracks from forming in the cake.

For an explanation of how to remove the cake from the springform, see page 19.

MOTHER WONDERFUL'S
HONEY FIG CHEESECAKE

Preheat oven to 350° F.
Ingredients need not be at room temperature.

Crust

10″ SPRINGFORM		8″ SPRINGFORM
¼ pound (1 stick)	Lightly salted butter	4 tablespoons (½ stick)
2 cups	Finely ground vanilla wafer crumbs	1 cup + 2 tablespoons
¼ cup	Sugar	2 tablespoons

Melt butter over very low heat. Combine butter with crumbs and sugar in a food processor or with a fork until thoroughly blended. Press small amounts of crumb mix all the way up the sides of an ungreased 10-inch springform (2 inches up the sides of an ungreased 8-inch springform) and then press remaining crumb mix over bottom of springform. For a more detailed explanation of how to blend and lay down the crust, see pages 17-18.

Filling

10″ SPRINGFORM		8″ SPRINGFORM
2 pounds (four 8-ounce packages	Cream cheese	*1 pound (two 8-ounce packages)*
1 cup	Sugar	*½ cup*
1 teaspoon	Rose-petal water*	*½ teaspoon*
1 teaspoon	Orange-flower water*	*½ teaspoon*
1 teaspoon	Fresh lemon juice	*½ teaspoon*
¼ cup	Honey	*2 tablespoons*
pinch	Salt	*pinch*
4	Large eggs	*2*
4	Dried figs	*2*

*Rose-petal water and orange-flower water can be found in gourmet shops and Greek or Middle Eastern groceries. There is no substitute for them. They give the cake a very sensuous flavor. If they are unavailable in your town, they can be acquired by mail from The Spice Corner. See page 4 for mail-ordering information.

In a mixer, whip cream cheese on the highest speed for 5 minutes, then add sugar and beat for 2 minutes more. Add rose-petal water, orange-flower water, lemon juice, honey, and salt and blend thoroughly. Add the eggs, one at a time, keeping the mixer on the *lowest speed* in order to prevent too much air from destroying the proper consistency of the batter; mix just until each egg has been incorporated into the batter. Slice figs into thin slivers and fold into batter with a rubber spatula. *Or:*

If using a food processor, put the sugar in first. Cut each 8-ounce block of cream cheese into eight 1-inch cubes and add the first 8 cubes to bowl. Process using on-off pulse about 25 times, and then add the rest of the cream cheese cubes gradually, blending them in with on-off pulses until mixture is smooth and creamy. When you think it's perfect, blend nonstop for 20 seconds more, then blend in rose-petal water, orange-flower water, lemon juice, honey, and salt for 5 seconds. Crack eggs in a bowl, break them up slightly with a fork, add them to batter in processor bowl, and fold them lightly into batter with a rubber spatula to prevent them from sinking to the bottom. Cut the eggs into the batter by using the on-off pulse 10 times, then scrape down the sides with a rubber spatula and pulse on-off 5 times more. Cut figs into thin slivers and fold into batter with a rubber spatula.

Pour batter into crust and bake in preheated oven.

Baking Time

10″ SPRINGFORM	8″ SPRINGFORM
55 minutes	40 minutes

Remove from oven and let stand on a counter for 10 minutes while you prepare the glaze.

Sour Cream Glaze

10″ SPRINGFORM		8″ SPRINGFORM
2 cups	Sour cream	1 cup
1/4 cup	Sugar	2 tablespoons
1 teaspoon	Almond extract	1/2 teaspoon
2	Dried figs	2
1/4 cup	Chopped pistachios	2 tablespoons

Combine sour cream, sugar, and extract with a rubber spatula in a plastic bowl. Spread evenly and smoothly over top of baked filling. Slice figs into thin slivers and arrange fig strips vertically around the rim like the numbers on a clock face. Sprinkle with nuts and return to 350° F oven for 10 minutes. Remove from oven and *immediately* place in refrigerator to cool to prevent cracks from forming in the cake.

For an explanation of how to remove the cake from the spring-form, see page 19.

Optional but sensational

1 cup honey

1 cup sugar

2 cups water

1 teaspoon lemon juice

1 teaspoon orange-flower water

1 teaspoon rose-petal water

Combine all the above ingredients in a pan, bring to a boil, and then simmer for 20 minutes until the syrup thickens. Dribble 3 tablespoons of the syrup over the top of the cake 2 hours before serving. The remainder can be refrigerated until you make another honey fig cheesecake or can be used on ice cream or fruit.

MOTHER WONDERFUL'S
RASPBERRY TRIFLE CHEESECAKE

Preheat oven to 350° F.
Ingredients need not be at room temperature.

Crust

10″ SPRINGFORM		8″ SPRINGFORM
1/4 pound (1 stick)	Lightly salted butter	4 tablespoons (1/2 stick)
2 cups	Finely ground ladyfinger crumbs	1 cup + 2 tablespoons
1/4 cup	Sugar	2 tablespoons

Melt butter over very low heat. Combine butter with crumbs and sugar in a food processor or with a fork until thoroughly blended. Press small amounts of crust mix all the way up the sides of an ungreased 10-inch springform (2 inches up the sides of an ungreased 8-inch springform) and then press remaining crust mix over bottom of springform. For a more detailed explanation of how to blend and lay down the crust, see pages 17-18.

Filling

10″ SPRINGFORM		8″ SPRINGFORM
2 pounds (four 8-ounce packages)	Cream cheese	1 pound (two 8-ounce packages)
1 cup	Sugar	1/2 cup
1 1/2 teaspoons	Almond extract	3/4 teaspoon
1 tablespoon	Triple Sec	1 1/2 teaspoons

10″ SPRINGFORM		8″ SPRINGFORM
pinch	Salt	*pinch*
4	Large eggs	2
¼ *cup*	Blanched sliced almonds, toasted	*2 tablespoons*
⅓ *cup*	Raspberry preserves	*2¾ tablespoons*
½ *teaspoon*	Raspberry extract	*¼ teaspoon*

In a mixer, whip cream cheese on the highest setting for 5 minutes, then add sugar and whip for 2 minutes more. Add almond extract, Triple Sec, and salt and blend together thoroughly. Add the eggs, one at a time, keeping the mixer on the *lowest speed* in order to prevent too much air from destroying the proper consistency of the batter; mix just until each egg has been incorporated into the batter. *Or:*

If using a food processor, put the sugar in first. Cut each 8-ounce block of cream cheese into eight 1-inch cubes and add the first 8 cubes to bowl. Process using on-off pulse about 25 times, and then add the rest of the cream cheese cubes gradually, blending them in with on-off pulses until mixture is smooth and creamy. When you think it's perfect, blend nonstop for 20 seconds more. Add almond extract, Triple Sec, and salt and process for 10 seconds more. Crack eggs in a bowl, scramble them slightly with a fork, add them to batter in processor bowl, and fold them lightly into batter with a rubber spatula to prevent them from sinking to the bottom. Cut the eggs into the batter by using the on-off pulse 10 times, then scrape down the sides with a rubber spatula and pulse on-off 5 times more.

Remove 1 cup of batter (½ cup for 8-inch cake) and blend raspberry preserves and raspberry extract thoroughly into it with a rubber spatula. Blend the almonds into the remaining batter and pour into crust. Pour reserved batter into center of cake and cut through with a knife to achieve a swirl effect.

Bake in preheated oven.

Baking Time

10″ SPRINGFORM	8″ SPRINGFORM
1 hour and 10 minutes	50 minutes

Remove from oven and let stand on a counter for 10 minutes while you prepare the glaze.

Sour Cream Glaze

10″ SPRINGFORM		8″ SPRINGFORM
2 cups	Sour cream	1 cup
¼ cup	Sugar	2 tablespoons
1 teaspoon	Almond extract	½ teaspoon
¼ cup	Blanched, sliced almonds, toasted	2 tablespoons

Combine sour cream, sugar, and extract with a rubber spatula in a plastic bowl. Spread evenly and smoothly over top of baked filling, sprinkle with almonds, and return to 350° F oven for 10 minutes. Remove from oven and *immediately* place in refrigerator to cool. This prevents cracks from forming in the cake.

For an explanation of how to remove the cake from the springform, see page 19.

MOTHER WONDERFUL'S
RUM RAISIN CHEESECAKE

Preliminary

10″ SPRINGFORM		8″ SPRINGFORM
¹/₂ cup	Golden raisins	¹/₄ cup
¹/₂ cup	Dark raisins	¹/₄ cup
1 ¹/₂ tablespoons	Dark rum	2 ¹/₄ teaspoons

Soak raisins in rum.

Preheat oven to 350° F.
Ingredients need not be at room temperature.

Crust

10″ SPRINGFORM		8″ SPRINGFORM
¹/₄ pound (1 stick)	Lightly salted butter	4 tablespoons (¹/₂ stick)
2 cups	Finely ground vanilla wafer crumbs	1 cup + 2 tablespoons
¹/₄ cup	Sugar	2 tablespoons

Melt butter over very low heat. Combine butter with crumbs and sugar in a food processor or with a fork until thoroughly blended. Press small amounts of crust mix all the way up of the sides of an ungreased 10-inch springform (2 inches up the sides of an ungreased 8-inch springform) and then press remaining crust mix over bottom of springform. For a more detailed explanation of how to blend and lay down the crust, see pages 17-18.

Filling

10″ SPRINGFORM		8″ SPRINGFORM
2 pounds (four 8-ounce packages)	Cream cheese	*1 pound (two 8-ounce packages)*
1½ cups	Sugar	*¾ cup*
1 teaspoon	Vanilla extract	*½ teaspoon*
½ teaspoon	Rum extract	*¼ teaspoon*
pinch	Salt	*pinch*
1	Egg yolk	*½*
4	Large eggs	*2*

In a mixer, whip cream cheese on the highest speed for 5 minutes, then add sugar and beat for 2 minutes more. Add extracts and salt and blend thoroughly. Add the egg yolk and the eggs, one at a time, keeping the mixer on the *lowest speed* in order to prevent too much air from destroying the proper consistency of the batter; mix just until each egg has been incorporated into the batter. Fold in raisins and rum. *Or:*

If using a food processor, put the sugar in first. Cut each 8-ounce block of cream cheese into eight 1-inch cubes and add the first 8 cubes to bowl. Process using on-off pulse about 25 times, and then add the rest of the cream cheese cubes gradually, blending them in with on-off pulses until mixture is smooth and creamy. When you think it's perfect, blend nonstop for 20 seconds more, then blend in extracts and salt for 5 seconds. Crack eggs and yolk in a bowl, break them up slightly with a fork, add them to batter in processor bowl, and fold them lightly into batter with a rubber spatula to prevent them from sinking to the bottom. Cut the eggs into the batter by using the on-off pulse 10 times, then scrape down the sides with a rubber spatula and pulse on-off 5 times more. Fold in soaked raisins and rum.

Pour batter into crust and bake in preheated oven.

Baking Time

10″ SPRINGFORM	8″ SPRINGFORM
50 minutes	40 minutes

Remove from oven and let stand on a counter for 10 minutes while you prepare the glaze.

Sour Cream Glaze

10″ SPRINGFORM		8″ SPRINGFORM
2 cups	Sour cream	1 cup
1/4 cup	Sugar	2 tablespoons
1 teaspoon	Dark rum	1/2 teaspoon

Combine sour cream, sugar, and rum with rubber spatula in a plastic bowl. Spread evenly and smoothly over top of baked filling. Return to 350° F oven for 10 minutes. Remove from oven and *immediately* place in refrigerator to cool to prevent cracks from forming in the cake.

For an explanation of how to remove the cake from the springform, see page 19.

MOTHER WONDERFUL'S
SOUTHERN PEACH CHEESECAKE

Preheat oven to 350° F.
Ingredients need not be at room temperature.

Crust

10″ SPRINGFORM		8″ SPRINGFORM
1/4 pound (1 stick)	Lightly salted butter	4 tablespoons (1/2 stick)
1 1/2 cups	Finely ground vanilla wafer crumbs	3/4 cup + 2 tablespoons
1/2 cup	Finely chopped pecans	1/4 cup
1/4 cup	Sugar	2 tablespoons

Melt butter over very low heat. Combine butter with crumbs, nuts, and sugar in a food processor or with a fork until thoroughly blended. Press small amounts of crust mix all the way up the sides of an ungreased 10-inch springform (2 inches up the sides of an ungreased 8-inch springform) and then press remaining crust mix over bottom of springform. For a more detailed explanation of how to blend and lay down the crust, see pages 17-18.

Filling

10″ SPRINGFORM		8″ SPRINGFORM
2 pounds (four 8-ounce packages)	Cream cheese	*1 pound (two 8-ounce packages)*
1 cup	Sugar	*½ cup*
1 tablespoon	Peach extract	*1½ teaspoons*
1½ teaspoons	Vanilla extract	*¾ teaspoon*
pinch	Salt	*pinch*
4	Large eggs	*2*
½ cup	Peach preserves	*¼ cup*
½ cup	Grated coconut	*¼ cup*
½ cup	Chopped pecans	*¼ cup*

In a mixer, whip cream cheese on the highest speed for 5 minutes, then add sugar and beat for 2 minutes more. Add extracts and salt and blend together thoroughly. Add the eggs, one at a time, keeping the mixer on the *lowest speed* in order to prevent too much air from destroying the proper consistency of the batter; mix just until each egg has been incorporated into the batter. *Or:*

If using a food processor, put the sugar in first. Cut each 8-ounce block of cream cheese into eight 1-inch cubes and add the first 8 cubes to bowl. Process using on-off pulse about 25 times, and then add the rest of the cream cheese cubes gradually, blending them in with on-off pulses until mixture is smooth and creamy. When you think it's perfect, blend nonstop for 20 seconds more, then blend in extracts and salt for 5 seconds. Crack eggs in a bowl, break them up slightly with a fork, add them to batter in processor bowl and fold them lightly into batter with a rubber spatula to prevent them from sinking to the bottom. Cut the eggs into the batter by using the on-off pulse 10 times, then scrape down the sides with a rubber spatula and pulse on-off 5 times more.

Reserve 1 cup of batter (½ cup for 8-inch cake). Fold pecans into remaining batter with a rubber spatula and pour half of this batter into crust. Blend peach preserves and coconut into the reserved cup of batter and spread this in a layer over the batter in the crust. Cover with remaining batter.

Bake in preheated oven.

Baking Time

10″ SPRINGFORM	8″ SPRINGFORM
1 hour + 10 minutes	45 minutes

Remove from oven and let stand on a counter for 10 minutes while you prepare the glaze.

Sour Cream Glaze

10″ SPRINGFORM		8″ SPRINGFORM
2 cups	Sour cream	1 cup
1/4 cup	Sugar	2 tablespoons
1 teaspoon	Almond extract	1/2 teaspoon
2 tablespoons	Chopped pecans	1 to 2 tablespoons

Combine sour cream, sugar, and extract with a rubber spatula in a plastic bowl. Spread evenly and smoothly over top of baked filling, sprinkle with pecans, and return to 350° F oven for 10 minutes. Remove from oven and *immediately* place in refrigerator to cool to prevent cracks from forming in the cake.

For an explanation of how to remove the cake from the springform, see page 19.

NEW FLAVOR!

MOTHER WONDERFUL'S
STRAWBERRY CHEESECAKE

Preheat oven to 350° F.
Ingredients need not be at room temperature.

Crust

10″ SPRINGFORM		8″ SPRINGFORM
¼ *pound (1 stick)*	Lightly salted butter	*4 tablespoons (½ stick)*
2 cups	Finely ground tea biscuit crumbs	*1 cup + 2 tablespoons*
¼ *cup*	Sugar	*2 tablespoons*

Melt butter over very low heat. Combine butter with crumbs and sugar in a food processor or with a fork until thoroughly blended. Press small amounts of crumb mix all the way up the sides of an ungreased 10-inch springform (2 inches up the sides of an ungreased 8-inch springform) and then press remaining crumb mix over bottom of springform. For a more detailed explanation of how to blend and lay down the crust, see pages 17-18.

Filling

10" SPRINGFORM		8" SPRINGFORM
1 pint	Fresh strawberries	1/2 pint
as needed	Fruit Fresh*	as needed
2 pounds (four 8-ounce packages)	Cream cheese	1 pound (two 8-ounce packages)
2 cups	Sugar	1 cup
2 tablespoons	Strawberrry liqueur	1 tablespoon
1 teaspoon	Strawberry extract	1/2 teaspoon
pinch	Salt	pinch
4	Large eggs	2

*Fruit Fresh is a fruit "protector;" its main ingredients are dextrose (corn sugar) and ascorbic acid (Vitamin C).

Reserve a few of the most beautiful strawberries to decorate the cake. Remove the stems from the rest, cut into quarters, and sprinkle with Fruit Fresh to stop them from turning brown.

In a mixer, whip cream cheese on the highest speed for 5 minutes, then add sugar and whip for 2 minutes more. Add liqueur, extract, and salt and blend together thoroughly. Add the eggs, one at a time, keeping the mixer on the *lowest speed* in order to prevent too much air from destroying the proper consistency of the batter; mix just until each egg has been incorporated into the batter. Fold in quartered strawberries. *Or:*

If using a food processor, put the sugar in first. Cut each 8-ounce block of cream cheese into eight 1-inch cubes and add the first 8 cubes to bowl. Process using on-off pulse about 25 times, and then add the rest of the cream cheese cubes gradually, blending them in with on-off pulses until mixture is smooth and creamy. When you think it's perfect, blend nonstop for 20 seconds more, then blend in liqueur, extract, and salt for 10 seconds. Crack eggs in a bowl, break them up slightly with a fork, add them to batter in processor bowl, and fold them lightly into batter with a rubber spatula to prevent them from sinking to the bottom. Cut the eggs into the batter by using the on-off pulse 10 times, then scrape down the sides with a rubber spatula, and pulse on-off 5 times more. Fold cut strawberries in with a rubber spatula.

Pour batter into crust and bake in preheated oven.

Baking Time

10″ SPRINGFORM	8″ SPRINGFORM
1 hour	40 minutes

Remove from oven and let stand on a counter for 10 minutes while you prepare the glaze.

Sour Cream Glaze

10″ SPRINGFORM		8″ SPRINGFORM
2 cups	Sour cream	1 cup
1/4 cup	Sugar	2 tablespoons
1 teaspoon	Triple Sec or strawberry liqueur	1/2 teaspoon
	Reserved strawberries	

Combine sour cream, sugar, and liqueur with a rubber spatula in a plastic bowl. Spread evenly and smoothly over top of baked filling. Return to 350° F oven for 10 minutes. Remove from oven and *immediately* place in refrigerator to cool to prevent cracks from forming in the cake. When the outside is cool, decorate with reserved whole strawberries.

For an explanation of how to remove the cake from the springform, see page 19.

NEW FLAVOR!

MOTHER WONDERFUL'S
SPICY PLUM CHEESECAKE

Preheat oven to 350° F.
Ingredients need not be at room temperature.

Crust

10″ SPRINGFORM		8″ SPRINGFORM
1/4 pound (1 stick)	Lightly salted butter	4 tablespoons (1/2 stick)
1 1/2 cups	Finely ground vanilla wafer crumbs	3/4 cup
1/2 cup	Finely chopped pecans	1/4 cup + 2 tablespoons
1/4 cup	Sugar	2 tablespoons
1 teaspoon	Cinnamon	1/2 teaspoon

Melt butter over very low heat. Combine butter with crumbs, nuts, sugar, and cinnamon in a food processor or with a fork until thoroughly blended. Press small amounts of crust mix all the way up the sides of an ungreased 10-inch springform (2 inches up the sides of an ungreased 8-inch springform) and then press remaining crust mix over bottom of springform. For a more detailed explanation of how to blend and lay down the crust, see pages 17-18.

Filling

10″ SPRINGFORM		8″ SPRINGFORM
16-ounce can	Purple plums	*8-ounce can*
½ cup	Chopped pecans	*¼ cup*
½ teaspoon	Ground ginger	*¼ teaspoon*
½ teaspoon	Cinnamon	*¼ teaspoon*
⅛ teaspoon	Nutmeg	*4 pinches*
⅛ teaspoon	Alkermes* (optional)	*3 drops*
2 pounds (four 8-ounce packages)	Cream cheese	*1 pound (two 8-ounce packages)*
1¾ cups	Sugar	*¾ cup + 2 tablespoons*
1 tablespoon	Dark rum	*1½ teaspoons*
pinch	Salt	*pinch*
4	Large eggs	*2*

*This interesting flavoring is described on page 4.

Drain, halve, and pit the plums. Reserve 4 halves for garnish and blot excess liquid from them. Slice or dice the remaining plums, mix with nuts, ginger, cinnamon, nutmeg, and optional alkermes, and reserve.

In a mixer, whip cream cheese on the highest speed for 5 minutes, then add sugar and beat for 2 minutes more. Add rum and salt and blend together thoroughly. Add the eggs, one at a time, keeping the mixer on the *lowest speed* in order to prevent too much air from destroying the proper consistency of the batter; mix just until each egg has been incorporated into the batter. Fold in plum mixture with a rubber spatula. Or:

If using a food processor, put the sugar in first. Cut each 8-ounce block of cream cheese into eight 1-inch cubes and add the first 8 cubes to bowl. Process using on-off pulse about 25 times, andthen add the rest of the cream cheese cubes gradually, blending them in with on-off pulses until mixture is smooth and creamy. When you think it's perfect, blend nonstop for 20 seconds more, then blend in rum and salt for 10 seconds. Crack eggs in a bowl, break them up slightly with a fork, add them to batter in processor bowl, and fold them lightly into batter with a rubber spatula to prevent them from sinking to the bottom. Cut the eggs into the batter by using the on-off pulse 10 times, then scrape down the sides with a rubber spatula, and pulse on-off 5 times more. Fold in plum mixture with a rubber spatula.

Pour filling into crust and bake in preheated oven.

Baking Time

10″ SPRINGFORM	8″ SPRINGFORM
1 hour + 10 minutes	45 minutes

Remove from oven and let stand on a counter for 10 minutes while you prepare the glaze.

Sour Cream Glaze

10″ SPRINGFORM		8″ SPRINGFORM
2 cups	Sour cream	1 cup
1/4 cup	Sugar	2 tablespoons
1 teaspoon	Dark rum	1/2 teaspoon
	Reserved plum halves	
1/4 cup	Grated coconut	2 tablespoons

Combine sour cream, sugar, and rum with a rubber spatula in a plastic bowl. Spread evenly and smoothly over top of baked filling, decorate with plum halves, sprinkle with coconut, and return to 350° F oven for 10 minutes. Remove from oven and *immediately* place in refrigerator to cool to prevent cracks from forming in the cake.

For an explanation of how to remove the cake from the spring-form, see page 19.

MOTHER WONDERFUL'S
MUNICH CHEESECAKE

Preheat oven to 350° F.
Ingredients need not be at room temperature.

This cheesecake has no crust.
The bottom is the springform itself, which must be greased.

Filling

10″ SPRINGFORM		8″ SPRINGFORM
3 pounds (six 8-ounce packages)	Cream cheese	1½ pounds (three 8-ounce packages)
2 cups	Sugar	1 cup
1 tablespoon	Fresh lime juice	1½ teaspoons
1 tablespoon	Orange extract	1½ teaspoons
pinch	Salt	pinch
6	Large eggs	3

In a mixer, whip cream cheese on the highest speed for 5 minutes, then add sugar and beat for 2 minutes more. Add lime juice, extract, and salt and blend together thoroughly. Add the eggs, one at a time, keeping the mixer on the *lowest speed* in order to prevent too much air from destroying the proper consistency of the batter; mix just until each egg has been incorporated into the batter. *Or:*

If using a food processor, put the sugar in first. Cut each 8-ounce block of cream cheese into eight 1-inch cubes and add the first 8 cubes to bowl. Process using on-off pulse about 25 times, and then add the rest of the cream cheese cubes gradually, blending them in with on-off pulses until mixture is smooth and creamy. When you think it's perfect, blend nonstop for 20 seconds more, then blend in lime juice, extract, and salt for 5 seconds. Crack eggs in a bowl, break them up slightly with a fork, add them to batter in processor bowl, and fold them lightly into batter with a rubber spatula to prevent them from sinking to the bottom. Cut the eggs into the batter by using the on-off pulse 10 times, then scrape down the sides with a rubber spatula and pulse on-off 5 times more.

Pour batter into greased pan and bake in preheated oven.

Baking Time

10″ SPRINGFORM	8″ SPRINGFORM
1 hour + 10 minutes	50 minutes

Remove from oven and let stand on a counter for 10 minutes while you prepare the nut-top crust.

Nut-Top Crust

10″ SPRINGFORM		8″ SPRINGFORM
1 cup	Chopped walnuts	1/2 cup
1/4 cup	Flour	2 tablespoons
1/4 cup (1/2 stick)	Lightly salted butter, softened	2 tablespoons
1/2 teaspoon	Cinnamon	1/4 teaspoon
1/2 cup	Brown sugar, firmly packed	1/4 cup
1/2 cup	White raisins	1/4 cup

Combine walnuts, flour, butter, cinnamon, and brown sugar in food processor until well blended. Mix raisins in with a spoon. Coat baked cheesecake with walnut mixture and return to 350° F oven for 10 minutes. Remove from oven and *immediately* place in refrigerator to cool to prevent cracks from forming in the cake.

To remove cake from springform, loosen springform clasp; if necessary, separate cake from sides with a sharp knife or a metal spatula, put a serving plate on top of the springform, and turn cake and pan upside down, so the nut topping will be on the bottom.

MOTHER WONDERFUL'S
BUTTERNUT CHEESECAKE

Preheat oven to 350° F.
Ingredients need not be at room temperature.

Crust

10″ SPRINGFORM		8″ SPRINGFORM
¼ *pound (1 stick)*	Lightly salted butter	*4 tablespoons (½ stick)*
2 cups	Finely ground vanilla wafer crumbs	*1 cup + 2 tablespoons*
¼ *cup*	Sugar	*2 tablespoons*

Melt butter over very low heat. Combine butter with crumbs and sugar in a food processor or with a fork until thoroughly blended. Press small amounts of crumb mix all the way up the sides of an ungreased 10-inch springform (2 inches up the sides of an ungreased 8-inch springform) and then press remaining crumb mix over bottom of springform. For a more detailed explanation of how to blend and lay down the crust, see pages 17-18.

Filling

10″ SPRINGFORM		8″ SPRINGFORM
6 ounces	Butterscotch bits	3 ounces
2 pounds (four 8-ounce packages)	Cream cheese	1 pound (two 8-ounce packages)
1 1/4 cups	Sugar	1/2 cup + 2 tablespoons
1 1/2 tablespoons	Dark rum	2 1/4 teaspoons
1/2 cup	Chopped pecans	1/4 cup
pinch	Salt	pinch
4	Large eggs	2

Melt butterscotch bits over simmering water in the top of a double boiler, in a pan over a heat diffuser, or in a microwave oven and reserve.

In a mixer, whip cream cheese on the highest speed for 5 minutes, then add sugar and beat for 2 minutes more. Add melted butterscotch bits, rum, pecans, and salt and blend thoroughly. Add the eggs, one at a time, keeping the mixer on the lowest speed in order to prevent too much air from destroying the proper consistency of the batter; mix just until each egg has been incorporated into the batter. Or:

If using a food processor, put the sugar in first. Cut each 8-ounce block of cream cheese into eight 1-inch cubes and add the first 8 cubes to bowl. Process using on-off pulse about 25 times, and then add the rest of the cream cheese cubes gradually, blending them in with on-off pulses until mixture is smooth and creamy. When you think it's perfect, blend nonstop for 20 seconds more, then blend in melted butterscotch bits, rum, pecans, and salt for 5 seconds. Crack eggs in a bowl, break them up slightly with a fork, add them to batter in processor bowl, and fold them lightly into batter with a rubber spatula to prevent them from sinking to the bottom. Cut the eggs into the batter by using the on-off pulse 10 times, then scrape down the sides with a rubber spatula and pulse on-off 5 times more.

Pour batter into crust and bake in preheated oven.

Baking Time

10″ SPRINGFORM	8″ SPRINGFORM
55 minutes	40 minutes

Remove from oven and let stand on a counter for 10 minutes while you prepare the glaze.

Sour Cream Glaze

10″ SPRINGFORM		8″ SPRINGFORM
2 cups	Sour cream	*1 cup*
¼ cup	Sugar	*2 tablespoons*
1 teaspoon	Dark rum	*½ teaspoon*
3 tablespoons	Chopped pecans	*2 tablespoons*

Combine sour cream, sugar, and rum with a rubber spatula in a plastic bowl. Spread evenly and smoothly over top of baked filling and sprinkle pecans over top. Return to 350° F oven for 10 minutes. Remove from oven and *immediately* place in refrigerator to cool to prevent cracks from forming in the cake.

For an explanation of how to remove the cake from the springform, see page 19.

MOTHER WONDERFUL'S
MAPLE WALNUT CHEESECAKE

Preheat oven to 350° F.
Ingredients need not be at room temperature.

Crust

10″ SPRINGFORM		8″ SPRINGFORM
¼ pound (1 stick)	Lightly salted butter	4 tablespoons (½ stick)
1½ cups	Finely ground vanilla wafer crumbs	¾ cup + 1 tablespoon
½ cup	Finely chopped walnuts	¼ cup + 1 tablespoon
¼ cup	Sugar	2 tablespoons

Melt butter over very low heat. Combine butter with crumbs, nuts, and sugar in a food processor or with a fork until thoroughly blended. Press small amounts of crust mix all the way up the sides of an ungreased 10-inch springform (2 inches up the sides of an ungreased 8-inch springform) and then press remaining crust mix over bottom of springform.

For a more detailed explanation of how to blend and lay down the crust, see pages 17-18.

Filling

10″ SPRINGFORM		8″ SPRINGFORM
2 pounds (four 8-ounce packages)	Cream cheese	*1 pound (two 8-ounce packages)*
1 1/3 cups	Sugar	*1/2 cup + 3 tablespoons*
1 teaspoon	Vanilla extract	*1/2 teaspoon*
1 teaspoon	Maple extract	*1/2 teaspoon*
1/4 cup	Maple syrup (fancy grade)	*2 tablespoons*
1/2 cup	Chopped walnuts	*1/4 cup*
pinch	Salt	*pinch*
4	Large eggs	*2*

In a mixer, whip cream cheese on the highest speed for 5 minutes, then add sugar and beat for 2 minutes more. Add extracts, maple syrup, walnuts, and salt and blend thoroughly. Add the eggs, one at a time, keeping the mixer on the *lowest speed* in order to prevent too much air from destroying the proper consistency of the batter; mix just until each egg has been incorporated into the batter. *Or:*

If using a food processor, put the sugar in first. Cut each 8-ounce block of cream cheese into eight 1-inch cubes and add the first 8 cubes to bowl. Process using on-off pulse about 25 times, and then add the rest of the cream cheese cubes gradually, blending them in with on-off pulses until mixture is smooth and creamy. When you think it's perfect, blend nonstop for 20 seconds more, then blend in extracts, syrup, walnuts, and salt for 5 seconds. Crack eggs in a bowl, break them up slightly with a fork, add them to batter in processor bowl, and fold them lightly into batter with a rubber spatula to prevent them from sinking to the bottom. Cut the eggs into the batter by using the on-off pulse 10 times, then scrape down the sides with a rubber spatula and pulse on-off 5 times more.

Pour batter into crust and bake in preheated oven.

Baking time

10″ SPRINGFORM	8″ SPRINGFORM
50 minutes	40 minutes

Remove from oven and let stand on a counter for 10 minutes while you prepare the glaze.

Sour Cream Glaze

10″ SPRINGFORM		8″ SPRINGFORM
2 cups	Sour cream	1 cup
1/4 cup	Sugar	2 tablespoons
1/2 teaspoon	Vanilla extract	1/4 teaspoon
2 tablespoons	Chopped walnuts	2 tablespoons

Combine sour cream, sugar, and extract with a rubber spatula in a plastic bowl. Spread evenly and smoothly over top of baked filling and sprinkle with walnuts. Return to 350° F oven for 10 minutes. Remove from oven and *immediately* place in refrigerator to cool to prevent cracks from forming in the cake.

For an explanation of how to remove the cake from the springform, see page 19.

MOTHER WONDERFUL'S
HAZELNUT CHEESECAKE

Preheat oven to 350° F.
Ingredients need not be at room temperature.

Preliminary

10″ SPRINGFORM		8″ SPRINGFORM
1 cup + 2 tablespoons	Ground hazelnuts (filberts)	½ cup + 1 tablespoon

Put nuts on a pan and toast in a 350° F oven for 5 to 10 minutes, watching carefully to make sure they do not burn.

Crust

10″ SPRINGFORM		8″ SPRINGFORM
¼ pound (1 stick)	Lightly salted butter	4 tablespoons (½ stick)
1½ cups	Finely ground vanilla wafer crumbs	¾ cup + 2 tablespoons
½ cup	Ground toasted hazelnuts	¼ cup
¼ cup	Sugar	2 tablespoons

Melt butter over very low heat. Combine butter with crumbs, nuts, and sugar in a food processor or with a fork until thoroughly blended. Press small amounts of crust mix all the way up the sides of an ungreased 10-inch springform (2 inches up the sides of an ungreased 8-inch springform) and then press remaining crust mix over bottom of springform. For a more detailed explanation of how to blend and lay down the crust, see pages 17-18.

Filling

10″ SPRINGFORM		8″ SPRINGFORM
2 pounds (four 8-ounce packages)	Cream cheese	1 pound (two 8-ounce packages)
1 1/2 cups	Sugar	3/4 cup
2 tablespoons	Frangelico liqueur (my preference) or praline liqueur	1 tablespoon
1/2 cup	Ground toasted hazelnuts	1/4 cup
pinch	Salt	pinch
4	Large eggs	2

In a mixer, whip cream cheese on the highest speed for 5 minutes, then add sugar and beat for 2 minutes more. Add liqueur, hazelnuts, and salt and blend together thoroughly. Add the eggs, one at a time, keeping the mixer on the *lowest speed* in order to prevent too much air from destroying the proper consistency of the batter; mix just until each egg has been incorporated into the batter. *Or:*

If using a food processor, put the sugar in first. Cut each 8-ounce block of cream cheese into eight 1-inch cubes and add the first 8 cubes to bowl. Process using on-off pulse about 25 times, and then add the rest of the cream cheese cubes gradually, blending them in with on-off pulses until mixture is smooth and creamy. When you think it's perfect, blend nonstop for 20 seconds more, then blend in liqueur, hazelnuts, and salt for 5 seconds. Crack eggs in a bowl, break them up slightly with a fork, add them to batter in processor bowl, and fold them lightly into batter with a rubber spatula to prevent them from sinking to the bottom. Cut the eggs into the batter by using the on-off pulse 10 times, then scrape down the sides with a rubber spatula and pulse on-off 5 times more.

Pour batter into crust and bake in preheated oven.

Baking Time

10" SPRINGFORM	8" SPRINGFORM
55 minutes	40 minutes

Remove from oven and let stand on a counter for 10 minutes while you prepare the glaze.

Sour Cream Glaze

10" SPRINGFORM		8" SPRINGFORM
2 cups	Sour cream	1 cup
1/4 cup	Sugar	2 tablespoons
1 teaspoon	Frangelico or praline liqueur	1/2 teaspoon
2 tablespoons	Ground toasted hazelnuts	1 tablespoon

Combine sour cream, sugar, and liqueur with a rubber spatula in a plastic bowl. Spread evenly and smoothly over top of baked filling, sprinkle with hazelnuts, and return to 350° F oven for 10 minutes. Remove from oven and *immediately* place in refrigerator to cool to prevent cracks from forming in the cake.

For an explanation of how to remove the cake from the springform, see page 19.

MOTHER WONDERFUL'S
PRALINE CHEESECAKE

Preheat oven to 350° F.
Ingredients need not be at room temperature.

Crust

10″ SPRINGFORM		8″ SPRINGFORM
¼ *pound (1 stick)*	Lightly salted butter	*4 tablespoons (½ stick)*
1 cup	Finely ground vanilla wafer crumbs	*½ cup + 2 tablespoons*
1 cup	Finely chopped pecans	*½ cup*
2 tablespoons	White sugar	*1 tablespoon*
2 tablespoons	Brown sugar, firmly packed	*1 tablespoon*

Melt butter over very low heat. Combine butter with crumbs, nuts, and sugars in a food processor or with a fork until thoroughly blended. Press small amounts of crust mix all the way up the sides of an ungreased 10-inch springform (2 inches up the sides of an ungreased 8-inch springform) and then press remaining crust mix over bottom of springform. For a more detailed explanation of how to blend and lay down the crust, see pages 17-18.

Filling

10″ SPRINGFORM		8″ SPRINGFORM
2 pounds (four 8-ounce packages)	Cream cheese	1 pound (two 8-ounce packages)
3/4 cup	White sugar	6 tablespoons
3/4 cup	Brown sugar, firmly packed	6 tablespoons
1 1/2 tablespoons	Praline liqueur or dark rum	2 1/4 teaspoons
1/2 cup	Pecan brittle or cashew brittle, chopped	1/4 cup
pinch	Salt	pinch
4	Large eggs	2

In a mixer, whip cream cheese on the highest speed for 5 minutes, then add sugars and beat for 2 minutes more. Add liqueur, brittle, and salt and blend together thoroughly. Add the eggs one at a time, keeping the mixer on the *lowest speed* in order to prevent too much air from destroying the proper consistency of the batter; mix just until each egg has been incorporated into the batter. *Or:*

If using a food processor, put the sugar in first. Cut each 8-ounce block of cream cheese into eight 1-inch cubes and add the first 8 cubes to bowl. Process using on-off pulse about 25 times, and then add the rest of the cream cheese cubes gradually, blending them in with on-off pulses until mixture is smooth and creamy. When you think it's perfect, blend nonstop for 20 seconds more, then blend in liqueur, brittle, and salt for 5 seconds. Crack eggs in a bowl, break them up slightly with a fork, add them to batter in processor bowl, and fold them lightly into batter with a rubber spatula to prevent them from sinking to the bottom. Cut the eggs into the batter by using the on-off pulse 10 times, then scrape down the sides with a rubber spatula and pulse on-off 5 times more.

Pour batter into crust and bake in preheated oven.

Baking time

10″ SPRINGFORM	8″ SPRINGFORM
50 minutes	40 minutes

Remove from oven and let stand on a counter for 10 minutes while you prepare the glaze.

Sour Cream Glaze

10″ SPRINGFORM		8″ SPRINGFORM
2 cups	Sour cream	1 cup
1/4 cup	Brown sugar, firmly packed	2 tablespoons
1 teaspoon	Praline liqueur or dark rum	1/2 teaspoon
1/2 teaspoon	Maple syrup	1/4 teaspoon
as needed	Pecan or cashew brittle, chopped	as needed

Combine sour cream, sugar, liqueur, and syrup with a rubber spatula in a plastic bowl. Spread evenly and smoothly over top of baked filling, sprinkle with chopped brittle, and return to 350° F oven for 10 minutes. Remove from oven and *immediately* place in refrigerator to cool to prevent cracks from forming in the cake.

For an explanation of how to remove the cake from the springform, see page 19.

MOTHER WONDERFUL'S
NUT SUNDAE CHEESECAKE

Preheat oven to 350° F.
Ingredients need not be at room temperature.

Crust

10″ SPRINGFORM		8″ SPRINGFORM
1/4 pound (1 stick)	Lightly salted butter	*4 tablespoons (1/2 stick)*
2 cups	Finely ground vanilla wafer crumbs	*1 cup + 2 tablespoons*
1/4 cup	Sugar	*1 cup + 2 tablespoons*

Melt butter over very low heat. Combine butter with crumbs and sugar in a food processor or with a fork until thoroughly blended. Press small amounts of crumb mix all the way up the sides of an ungreased 10-inch springform (2 inches up the sides of an ungreased 8-inch springform) and then press remaining crumb mix over bottom of springform. For a more detailed explanation of how to blend and lay down the crust, see pages 17-18.

Filling

10" SPRINGFORM		8" SPRINGFORM
1½ pounds (three 8-ounce packages)	Cream cheese	12 ounces (one and a half 8-ounce packages)
1½ cups	Sugar	¾ cup
1 cup	Smooth peanut butter	½ cup
1 teaspoon	Vanilla extract	½ teaspoon
1½ tablespoons	Dark rum	2¼ teaspoons
pinch	Salt	pinch
4	Large eggs	2
¼ cup	Nutella* or fudge topping	2 tablespoons

*Nutella is a brand name for a delicious concoction of hazelnuts and chocolate. It's sometimes found in supermarkets. If you see it, grab it. There's another version of this that has chocolate and hazelnut side by side in a jar that looks like a beer glass. It's called Crumpy Duo. It's also mighty wonderful!

In a mixer, whip cream cheese on the highest speed for 5 minutes, then add sugar and peanut butter and beat for 2 minutes more. Add vanilla, rum, and salt and blend together thoroughly. Add the eggs, one at a time, keeping the mixer on the *lowest speed* in order to prevent too much air from destroying the proper consistency of the batter; mix just until each egg has been incorporated into the batter. *Or:*

If using a food processor, put the sugar in first. Cut each 8-ounce block of cream cheese into eight 1-inch cubes and add the first 8 cubes to bowl. Process using on-off pulse about 25 times, and then add the rest of the cream cheese cubes gradually, blending them in with on-off pulses until mixture is smooth and creamy. When you think it's perfect, blend nonstop for 20 seconds more, then blend in peanut butter, vanilla, rum, and salt for 5 seconds. Crack eggs in a bowl, break them up slightly with a fork, add them to batter in processor bowl, and fold them lightly into batter with a rubber spatula to prevent them from sinking to the bottom. Cut the eggs into the batter by using the on-off pulse 10 times, then scrape down the sides with a rubber spatula, and pulse on-off 5 times more.

Pour into crust. Warm bottle of Nutella or fudge topping under hot running water and dribble sauce over the top of the filling. Cut into the batter with a knife to achieve a swirl effect and bake in preheated oven.

Baking Time

10″ SPRINGFORM	8″ SPRINGFORM
55 minutes	40 minutes

Remove from oven and let stand on a counter for 10 minutes while you prepare the glaze.

Sour Cream Glaze

10″ SPRINGFORM		8″ SPRINGFORM
2 cups	Sour cream	1 cup
1/4 cup	Sugar	2 tablespoons
1 teaspoon	Vanilla	1/2 teaspoon
as needed	Nutella or fudge topping	as needed

Combine sour cream, sugar, and vanilla with a rubber spatula in a plastic bowl. Spread evenly and smoothly over top of baked filling. Dribble Nutella or fudge topping on glaze and make a decorative swirl design with the point of a knife. Return to 350° F oven for 10 minutes. Remove from oven and *immediately* place in refrigerator to cool to prevent cracks from forming in the cake.

For an explanation of how to remove the cake from the springform, see page 19.

MOTHER WONDERFUL'S
PEANUT BUTTER AND JELLY CHEESECAKE

Preheat oven to 350° F.
Ingredients need not be at room temperature.

Crust

10″ SPRINGFORM		8″ SPRINGFORM
1/4 pound (1 stick)	Lightly salted butter	4 tablespoons (1/2 stick)
1 1/2 cups	Finely ground crisp vanilla wafer crumbs	3/4 cup + 2 tablespoons
1/2 cup	Finely chopped peanuts	1/4 cup
1/4 cup	Sugar	2 tablespoons

Melt butter over very low heat. Combine butter with crumbs, peanuts, and sugar in a food processor or with a fork until thoroughly blended. Press small amounts of crumb mix all the way up the sides of an ungreased 10-inch springform (2 inches up the sides of an ungreased 8-inch springform) and then press remaining crumb mix over bottom of springform. For a more detailed explanation of how to blend and lay down the crust, see pages 17-18.

Filling

10″ SPRINGFORM		8″ SPRINGFORM
2 pounds (four 8-ounce packages)	Cream cheese	*1 pound (two 8-ounce packages)*
1 ¼ cups	Sugar	*½ cup + 2 tablespoons*
1 tablespoon	Dark rum	*1 ½ teaspoons*
1 ½ teaspoons	Vanilla extract	*¾ teaspoon*
pinch	Salt	*pinch*
4	Large eggs	*2*
⅓ cup	Raspberry preserves	*2¾ tablespoons*
¼ cup	Smooth peanut butter	*2 tablespoons*

In a mixer, whip cream cheese on the highest speed for 5 minutes, then add sugar and beat for 2 minutes more. Add rum, vanilla, and salt and blend together thoroughly. Add the eggs, one at a time, keeping the mixer on the *lowest speed* in order to prevent too much air from destroying the proper consistency of the batter; mix just until each egg has been incorporated into the batter. *Or:*

If using a food processor, put the sugar in first. Cut each 8-ounce block of cream cheese into eight 1-inch cubes and add the first 8 cubes to bowl. Process using on-off pulse about 25 times, and then add the rest of the cream cheese cubes gradually, blending them in with on-off pulses until mixture is smooth and creamy. When you think it's perfect, blend nonstop for 20 seconds more. Add rum, vanilla, and salt and process for 10 seconds more. Crack eggs in a bowl, break them up slightly with a fork, add them to batter in processor bowl, and fold them lightly into batter with a rubber spatula to prevent them from sinking to the bottom. Cut the eggs into the batter by using the on-off pulse 10 times, then scrape down the sides with a rubber spatula and pulse on-off 5 times more.

Remove 1 cup of batter (½ cup for 8-inch cake) and blend raspberry preserves thoroughly into it with a rubber spatula. Remove a second cup of batter (½ cup for 8-inch cake) and blend peanut butter thoroughly into it with a rubber spatula. Pour remaining batter into crust. Pour peanut-flavored batter into the center of the filling. Pour raspberry-flavored batter in a circle around the rim. Cut through both with a knife to achieve a swirl effect.

Pour batter into crust and bake in preheated oven.

Baking Time

10″ SPRINGFORM	8″ SPRINGFORM
50 minutes	40 minutes

Remove from oven and let stand on a counter for 10 minutes while you prepare the glaze.

Sour Cream Glaze

10″ SPRINGFORM		8″ SPRINGFORM
2 cups	Sour cream	1 cup
¼ cup	Sugar	2 tablespoons
1 teaspoon	Dark rum	½ teaspoon
2 tablespoons	Chopped peanuts	1 tablespoon

Combine sour cream, sugar, and rum with a rubber spatula in a plastic bowl. Spread evenly and smoothly over top of baked filling, sprinkle with chopped peanuts, and return to 350° F oven for 10 minutes. Remove from oven and *immediately* place in refrigerator to cool. This prevents cracks from forming in the cake.

For an explanation of how to remove the cake from the spring-form, see page 19.

MOTHER WONDERFUL'S
ANISEED CHEESECAKE

Preheat oven to 350° F.
Ingredients need not be at room temperature.

Crust

10″ SPRINGFORM		8″ SPRINGFORM
1/4 pound (1 stick)	Lightly salted butter	4 tablespoons (1/2 stick)
2 cups	Finely ground vanilla wafer crumbs	1 cup + 2 tablespoons
1/4 cup	Sugar	2 tablespoons

Melt butter over very low heat. Combine butter with crumbs and sugar in a food processor or with a fork until thoroughly blended. Press small amounts of crust mix all the way up the sides of an ungreased 10-inch springform (2 inches up the sides of an ungreased 8-inch springform) and then press remaining crust mix over bottom of springform. For a more detailed explanation of how to blend and lay down the crust, see pages 17-18.

Filling

10″ SPRINGFORM		8″ SPRINGFORM
2 pounds (four 8-ounce packages)	Cream cheese	1 pound (two 8-ounce packages
1½ cups	Sugar	¾ cup
1 tablespoon	Anisette	1½ teaspoons
2 teaspoons	Anise extract	1 teaspoon
¼ cup	Poppyseed pastry filling	2 teaspoons
½ cup	Pine nuts	¼ cup
pinch	Salt	pinch
4	Large eggs	2

In a mixer, whip cream cheese on the highest speed for 5 minutes, then add sugar and beat for 2 minutes more. Add anisette, extract, poppyseed filling, pine nuts, and salt and blend together thoroughly. Add the eggs, one at a time, keeping the mixer on the *lowest speed* in order to prevent too much air from destroying the proper consistency of the batter; mix just until each egg has been incorporated into the batter. *Or:*

If using a food processor, put the sugar in first. Cut each 8-ounce block of cream cheese into eight 1-inch cubes and add the first 8 cubes to bowl. Process using on-off pulse about 25 times, and then add the rest of the cream cheese cubes gradually, blending them in with on-off pulses until mixture is smooth and creamy. When you think it's perfect, blend nonstop for 20 seconds more, then blend in anisette, anise extract, poppyseed filling, and salt for 5 seconds. Crack eggs in a bowl, break them up slightly with a fork, add them to batter in processor bowl, and fold them lightly into batter with a rubber spatula to prevent them from sinking to the bottom. Cut the eggs into the batter by using the on-off pulse 10 times, then scrape down the sides with a rubber spatula and pulse on-off 5 times more. Fold in pine nuts with a rubber spatula.

Pour batter into crust and bake in preheated oven.

Baking Time

10″ SPRINGFORM	8″ SPRINGFORM
55 minutes	40 minutes

Remove from oven and let stand on a counter for 10 minutes while you prepare the glaze.

Sour Cream Glaze

10″ SPRINGFORM		8″ SPRINGFORM
2 cups	Sour cream	*1 cup*
¼ cup	Sugar	*2 tablespoons*
1 teaspoon	Anisette	*½ teaspoon*

Combine sour cream, sugar, and anisette with a rubber spatula in a plastic bowl. Spread evenly and smoothly over top of baked filling and return to 350° F oven for 10 minutes. Remove from oven and *immediately* place in refrigerator to cool to prevent cracks from forming in the cake.

For an explanation of how to remove the cake from the springform, see page 19.

MOTHER WONDERFUL'S
MOCHA CHEESECAKE

Preheat oven to 350° F.
Ingredients need not be at room temperature.

Crust

10″ SPRINGFORM		8″ SPRINGFORM
1/4 pound (1 stick)	Lightly salted butter	4 tablespoons (1/2 sticks)
2 cups	Finely ground crisp chocolate cookie crumbs	1 cup + 2 tablespoons
1/4 cup	Sugar	2 tablespoons

Melt butter over very low heat. Combine butter with crumbs and sugar in a food processor or with a fork until thoroughly blended. Press small amounts of crumb mix all the way up the sides of an ungreased 10-inch springform (2 inches up the sides of an ungreased 8-inch springform) and then press remaining crumb mix over bottom of springform. For a more detailed explanation of how to blend and lay down the crust, see pages 17-18.

Filling

10″ SPRINGFORM		8″ SPRINGFORM
4 ounces	Sweet chocolate	2 ounces
2 pounds (four 8-ounce packages)	Cream cheese	1 pound (two 8-ounce packages)
1 1/4 cups	Sugar	1/2 cup + 2 tablespoons
2 teaspoons	Instant espresso	1 teaspoon

10″ SPRINGFORM		8″ SPRINGFORM
2 tablespoons	White rum	*1 tablespoon*
pinch	Salt	*pinch*
4	Large eggs	2

Melt sweet chocolate over simmering water in the top of a double boiler, in a pan over a heat diffuser, or in a microwave oven and reserve.

In a mixer, whip cream cheese on the highest speed for 5 minutes, then add sugar and beat for 2 minutes more. Dissolve espresso in rum. Add with melted chocolate and salt to batter and blend together thoroughly. Add the eggs, one at a time, keeping the mixer on the *lowest speed* in order to prevent too much air from destroying the proper consistency of the batter; mix just until each egg has been incorporated into the batter. *Or:*

If using a food processor, put the sugar in first. Cut each 8-ounce block of cream cheese into eight 1-inch cubes and add the first 8 cubes to bowl. Process using on-off pulse about 25 times, and then add the rest of the cream cheese cubes gradually, blending them in with on-off pulses until mixture is smooth and creamy. When you think it's perfect, blend nonstop for 20 seconds more. Dissolve instant espresso in rum, then add to batter with melted chocolate and salt and process for 10 seconds more. Crack eggs in a bowl, break them up slightly with a fork, add them to batter in processor bowl, and fold them lightly into batter with a rubber spatula to prevent them from sinking to the bottom. Cut the eggs into the batter by using the on-off pulse 10 times, then scrape down the sides with a rubber spatula and pulse on-off 5 times more.

Pour batter into crust and bake in preheated oven.

Baking Time

10″ SPRINGFORM	8″ SPRINGFORM
50 minutes	40 minutes

Remove from oven and let stand on a counter for 10 minutes while you prepare the glaze.

Sour Cream Glaze

10" SPRINGFORM		8" SPRINGFORM
2 cups	Sour cream	1 cup
¼ cup	Sugar	2 tablespoons
1 teaspoon	White rum	½ teaspoon
as needed	Shaved coffee-flavored chocolate bar	as needed

Combine sour cream, sugar, and rum with a rubber spatula in a plastic bowl. Spread evenly and smoothly over top of baked filling and return to 350° F oven for 10 minutes. Remove from oven and *immediately* place in refrigerator to cool. This prevents cracks from forming in the cake. Before serving sprinkle top with shaved or grated coffee-flavored chocolate.

For an explanation of how to remove the cake from the springform, see page 19.

MOTHER WONDERFUL'S
MOCHA BLANCA CHEESECAKE

Preheat oven to 350° F.
Ingredients need not be at room temperature.

Crust

10″ SPRINGFORM		8″ SPRINGFORM
¼ pound (1 stick)	Lightly salted butter	4 tablespoons (½ stick)
2 cups	Finely ground crisp chocolate cookie crumbs	1 cup + 2 tablespoons
¼ cup	Sugar	2 tablespoons

Melt butter over very low heat. Combine butter with crumbs and sugar in a food processor or with a fork until thoroughly blended. Press small amounts of crumb mix all the way up the sides of an ungreased 10-inch springform (2 inches up the sides of an ungreased 8-inch springform) and then press remaining crust mix over bottom of springform. For a more detailed explanation of how to blend and lay down the crust, see pages 17-18.

Filling

10″ SPRINGFORM		8″ SPRINGFORM
3 ounces	White chocolate	1½ ounces
2 pounds (four 8-ounce packages)	Cream cheese	1 pound (two 8-ounce packages)
1¼ cups	Sugar	½ cup + 2 tablespoons
2 teaspoons	Instant espresso	1 teaspoon
1½ teaspoons	Coffee liqueur	¾ teaspoon
1 tablespoon	Fine cognac	1½ teaspoons
pinch	Salt	pinch
4	Large eggs	2

Melt white chocolate over simmering water in the top of a double boiler, in a pan over a heat diffuser, or in a microwave oven and reserve.

In a mixer, whip cream cheese on the highest speed for 5 minutes, then add sugar and beat for 2 minutes more. Dissolve espresso in coffee liqueur and cognac. Add with melted chocolate and salt to batter and blend together thoroughly. Add the eggs, one at a time, keeping the mixer on the lowest speed in order to prevent too much air from destroying the proper consistency of the batter; mix just until each egg has been incorporated into the batter. Or:

If using a food processor, put the sugar in first. Cut each 8-ounce block of cream cheese into eight 1-inch cubes and add the first 8 cubes to bowl. Process using on-off pulse about 25 times, and then add the rest of the cream cheese cubes gradually, blending them in with on-off pulses until mixture is smooth and creamy. When you think it's perfect, blend nonstop for 20 seconds more. Dissolve instant espresso in coffee liqueur and cognac, then add to batter with melted chocolate and salt and process for 10 seconds more. Crack eggs in a bowl, break them up slightly with a fork, add them to batter in processor bowl, and fold them lightly into batter with a rubber spatula to prevent them from sinking to the bottom. Cut the eggs into the batter by using the on-off pulse 10 times, then scrape down the sides with a rubber spatula and pulse on-off 5 times more.

Pour batter into crust and bake in preheated oven.

Baking Time

10″ SPRINGFORM	8″ SPRINGFORM
55 minutes	40 minutes

Remove from oven and let stand on a counter for 10 minutes while you prepare the glaze.

Sour Cream Glaze

10″ SPRINGFORM		8″ SPRINGFORM
2 cups	Sour cream	1 cup
1/4 cup	Sugar	2 tablespoons
1 teaspoon	Coffee liqueur	1/2 teaspoon
as needed	Shaved coffee-flavored chocolate bar	as needed

Combine sour cream, sugar, and coffee liqueur with a rubber spatula in a plastic bowl. Spread evenly and smoothly over top of baked filling and return to 350° F oven for 10 minutes. Remove from oven and *immediately* place in refrigerator to cool. This prevents cracks from forming in the cake. Before serving sprinkle top with shaved or grated coffee-flavored chocolate.

For an explanation of how to remove the cake from the springform, see page 19.

MOTHER WONDERFUL'S
JAMOCHA CHEESECAKE

Preheat oven to 350° F.
Ingredients need not be at room temperature.

Crust

10″ SPRINGFORM		8″ SPRINGFORM
¼ pound (1 stick)	Lightly salted butter	4 tablespoons (½ stick)
2 cups	Finely ground crisp chocolate cookie crumbs	1 cup + 2 tablespoons
¼ cup	Sugar	2 tablespoons

Melt butter over very low heat. Combine butter with crumbs and sugar in a food processor or with a fork until thoroughly blended. Press small amounts of crumb mix all the way up the sides of an ungreased 10-inch springform (2 inches up the sides of an ungreased 8-inch springform) and then press remaining crumb mix over bottom of springform. For a more detailed explanation of how to blend and lay down the crust, see pages 17-18.

Filling

10″ SPRINGFORM		8″ SPRINGFORM
4 ounces	Sweet chocolate	2 ounces
2 pounds (four 8-ounce packages)	Cream cheese	1 pound (two 8-ounce packages)
1½ cups	Sugar	¾ cup
1 teaspoon	Instant espresso	½ teaspoon

10″ SPRINGFORM		8″ SPRINGFORM
1 ½ *tablespoons*	Coffee liqueur	2 ¼ *teaspoons*
¼ *cup*	Chopped walnuts	2 *tablespoons*
pinch	Salt	*pinch*
4	Large eggs	2
⅓ *cup*	Chopped or grated sweet chocolate *or* chocolate chips	3 *tablespoons*

Melt 4 ounces (2 ounces for 8-inch cake) sweet chocolate over simmering water in the top of a double boiler, in a pan over a heat diffuser, or in a microwave oven, and reserve.

In a mixer, whip cream cheese on the highest speed for 5 minutes, then add sugar and beat for 2 minutes more. Dissolve espresso in coffee liqueur and then add with walnuts and salt to batter and blend together thoroughly. Add the eggs, one at a time, keeping the mixer on the *lowest speed* in order to prevent too much air from destroying the proper consistency of the batter; mix just until each egg has been incorporated into the batter. Fold in chopped chocolate or chocolate chips. *Or:*

If using a food processor, put the sugar in first. Cut each 8-ounce block of cream cheese into eight 1-inch cubes and add the first 8 cubes to bowl. Process using on-off pulse about 25 times, and then add the rest of the cream cheese cubes gradually, blending them in with on-off pulses until mixture is smooth and creamy. When you think it's perfect, blend nonstop for 20 seconds more. Dissolve instant espresso in coffee liqueur then add to batter with salt and process for 10 seconds more. Crack eggs in a bowl, break them up slightly with a fork, add them to batter in processor bowl, and fold them lightly into batter with a rubber spatula to prevent them from sinking to the bottom. Cut the eggs into the batter by using the on-off pulse 10 times, then scrape down the sides with a rubber spatula, add walnuts and chopped chocolate or chocolate chips and pulse on-off 5 times more.

Remove 1 cup of batter (½ cup for 8-inch cake) and reserve. Pour remainder of batter into crust. Add melted chocolate to the reserved batter and mix thoroughly with a rubber spatula. Pour into center of batter in pan and cut through with a knife to achieve a swirl effect, but with most of the chocolate remaining in the center of the cake. Save a bit of melted chocolate to use to decorate topping.

Pour batter into crust and bake in preheated oven.

Baking Time

10″ SPRINGFORM	8″ SPRINGFORM
1 hour + 10 minutes	45 minutes

Remove from oven and let stand on a counter for 10 minutes while you prepare the glaze.

Sour Cream Glaze

10″ SPRINGFORM		8″ SPRINGFORM
2 cups	Sour cream	1 cup
1/4 cup	Sugar	2 tablespoons
1 teaspoon	Coffee liqueur	1/2 teaspoon

Combine sour cream, sugar, and coffee liqueur with a rubber spatula in a plastic bowl. Spread evenly and smoothly over top of baked filling, decorate with swirls of remaining bits of melted chocolate, and return to 350° F oven for 10 minutes. Remove from oven and *immediately* place in refrigerator to cool. This prevents cracks from forming in the cake.

For an explanation of how to remove the cake from the springform, see page 19.

MOTHER WONDERFUL'S
IRISH COFFEE CHEESECAKE

Preheat oven to 350° F.
Ingredients need not be at room temperature.

Crust

10" SPRINGFORM		8" SPRINGFORM
1/4 pound (1 stick)	Lightly salted butter	4 tablespoons (1/2 stick)
1 1/2 cups	Finely ground crisp chocolate cookie crumbs	3/4 cup + 2 tablespoons
1/2 cup	Grated coffee-flavored chocolate	1/4 cup
1/4 cup	Sugar	2 tablespoons

Melt butter over very low heat. Combine butter with crumbs, chocolate, and sugar in a food processor or with a fork until thoroughly blended. Press small amounts of crumb mix all the way up the sides of an ungreased 10-inch springform (2 inches up the sides of an ungreased 8-inch springform) and then press remaining crumb mix over bottom of springform. For a more detailed explanation of how to blend and lay down the crust, see pages 17-18.

Filling

10" SPRINGFORM		8" SPRINGFORM
2 pounds (four 8-ounce packages)	Cream cheese	1 pound (two 8-ounce packages)
1½ cups	Sugar	¾ cup
2 teaspoons	Instant espresso	1 teaspoon
1½ tablespoons	Irish whiskey	2¼ teaspoons
½ teaspoon	Whiskey extract (optional)	¼ teaspoon
pinch	Salt	pinch
4	Large eggs	2
¼ cup	Grated coffee- or mocha-flavored chocolate	2 tablespoons

In a mixer, whip cream cheese on the highest speed for 5 minutes, then add sugar and beat for 2 minutes more. Dissolve espresso in whiskey and then add with extract, grated chocolate, and salt to batter and blend together thoroughly. Add the eggs, one at a time, keeping the mixer on the *lowest speed* in order to prevent too much air from destroying the proper consistency of the batter; mix just until each egg has been incorporated into the batter. Or:

If using a food processor, put the sugar in first. Cut each 8-ounce block of cream cheese into eight 1-inch cubes and add the first 8 cubes to bowl. Process using on-off pulse about 25 times, and then add the rest of the cream cheese cubes gradually, blending them in with on-off pulses until mixture is smooth and creamy. When you think it's perfect, blend nonstop for 20 seconds more. Dissolve instant espresso in whiskey, then add to batter with extract and salt and process for 10 seconds more. Crack eggs in a bowl, break them up slightly with a fork, add them to batter in processor bowl, and fold them lightly into batter with a rubber spatula to prevent them from sinking to the bottom. Cut the eggs into the batter by using the on-off pulse 10 times, then scrape down the sides with a rubber spatula and pulse on-off 5 times more. Fold in grated chocolate.

Pour batter into crust and bake in preheated oven.

Baking Time

10″ SPRINGFORM	8″ SPRINGFORM
55 minutes	40 minutes

Remove from oven and let stand on a counter for 10 minutes while you prepare the glaze.

Sour Cream Glaze

10″ SPRINGFORM		8″ SPRINGFORM
2 cups	Sour cream	1 cup
1/4 cup	Sugar	2 tablespoons
1 teaspoon	Coffee liqueur	1/2 teaspoon
as needed	Shaved coffee-flavored chocolate bar	as needed

Combine sour cream, sugar, and coffee liqueur with a rubber spatula in a plastic bowl. Spread evenly and smoothly over top of baked filling and return to 350° F oven for 10 minutes. Remove from oven and *immediately* place in refrigerator to cool. This prevents cracks from forming in the cake. Before serving sprinkle top with shaved or grated coffee-flavored chocolate.

For an explanation of how to remove the cake from the springform, see page 19.

MOTHER WONDERFUL'S
SOUTHERN COFFEE CHEESECAKE

Preheat oven to 350° F.
Ingredients need not be at room temperature.

Crust

10″ SPRINGFORM		8″ SPRINGFORM
1/4 pound (1 stick)	Lightly salted butter	4 tablespoons (1/2 stick)
2 cups	Finely ground vanilla wafer crumbs	1 cup + 2 tablespoons
1/4 cup	Sugar	2 tablespoons

Melt butter over very low heat. Combine butter with crumbs, and sugar in a food processor or with a fork until thoroughly blended. Press small amounts of crumb mix all the way up the sides of an ungreased 10-inch springform (2 inches up the sides of an ungreased 8-inch springform) and then press remaining crumb mix over bottom of springform. For a more detailed explanation of how to blend and lay down the crust, see pages 17-18.

Filling

10″ SPRINGFORM		8″ SPRINGFORM
2 ounces	White chocolate	1 ounce
2 pounds (four 8-ounce packages)	Cream cheese	1 pound (two 8-ounce packages)
1 1/2 cups	Sugar	3/4 cup
1 teaspoon	Instant espresso	1/2 teaspoon

10″ SPRINGFORM		8″ SPRINGFORM
1 1/2 tablespoons	Coffee liqueur	2 1/4 teaspoons
1/2 cup	Chopped pecans	1/4 cup
pinch	Salt	pinch
4	Large eggs	2

Melt white chocolate over simmering water in the top of a double boiler, in a pan over a heat diffuser, or in a microwave oven, and reserve.

In a mixer, whip cream cheese on the highest speed for 5 minutes, then add sugar and beat for 2 minutes more. Add espresso, liqueur, pecans, and salt and blend together thoroughly. Add the eggs one at a time, keeping the mixer on the *lowest speed* in order to prevent too much air from destroying the proper consistency of the batter; mix just until each egg has been incorporated into the batter. *Or:*

If using a food processor, put the sugar in first. Cut each 8-ounce block of cream cheese into eight 1-inch cubes and add the first 8 cubes to bowl. Process using on-off pulse about 25 times, and then add the rest of the cream cheese cubes gradually, blending them in with on-off pulses until mixture is smooth and creamy. When you think it's perfect, blend nonstop for 20 seconds more, then blend in espresso, liqueur, pecans, and salt for 5 seconds. Crack eggs in a bowl, break them up slightly with a fork, add them to batter in processor bowl, and fold them lightly into batter with a rubber spatula to prevent them from sinking to the bottom. Cut the eggs into the batter by using the on-off pulse 10 times, then scrape down the sides with a rubber spatula and pulse on-off 5 times more.

Remove 1 cup of batter (1/2 cup for 8-inch cake), blend melted white chocolate into it with a rubber spatula, and reserve. Pour 1/2 of remaining batter into crust. Spread reserved white chocolate batter over it, and then cover with remaining batter. Bake in preheated oven.

Baking Time

10″ SPRINGFORM	8″ SPRINGFORM
55 minutes	40 minutes

Remove from oven and let stand on a counter for 10 minutes while you prepare the glaze.

Sour Cream Glaze

10″ SPRINGFORM		8″ SPRINGFORM
2 cups	Sour cream	1 cup
¼ cup	Brown sugar, firmly packed	2 tablespoons
1 teaspoon	Coffee liqueur	½ teaspoon
2 tablespoons	Chopped pecans	1 tablespoon

Combine sour cream, sugar, and liqueur with a rubber spatula in a plastic bowl. Spread evenly and smoothly over top of baked filling, sprinkle with chopped pecans, and return to 350° F oven for 10 minutes. Remove from oven and *immediately* place in refrigerator to cool to prevent cracks from forming in the cake.

For an explanation of how to remove the cake from the springform, see page 19.

NEW FLAVOR!

MOTHER WONDERFUL'S
CAPPUCCINO SWIRL CHEESECAKE

Preheat oven to 350° F.
Ingredients need not be at room temperature.

Crust

10″ SPRINGFORM		8″ SPRINGFORM
¼ pound (1 stick)	Lightly salted butter	4 tablespoons (½ stick)
1 cup	Finely ground crisp chocolate cookie crumbs	½ cup
1 cup	Finely ground vanilla wafer crumbs	½ cup + 2 tablespoons
1 teaspoon	Mocha flavoring	½ teaspoon
¼ cup	Sugar	2 tablespoons

Melt butter over very low heat. Combine butter with crumbs, flavoring and sugar in a food processor or with a fork until thoroughly blended. Press small amounts of crumb mix all the way up the sides of an ungreased 10-inch springform (2 inches up the sides of an ungreased 8-inch springform) and then press remaining crumb mix over bottom of springform. For a more detailed explanation of how to blend and lay down the crust, see pages 17-18.

Filling

10" SPRINGFORM		8" SPRINGFORM
6 ounces	Sweet chocolate	3 ounces
2 pounds (four 8-ounce packages)	Cream cheese	1 pound (two 8-ounce packages)
1 1/2 cups	Sugar	3/4 cup
1 tablespoon	Instant espresso	1 1/2 teaspoons
1 1/2 teaspoons	Mocha flavoring	3/4 teaspoon
1 1/2 teaspoons	Light rum	3/4 teaspoon
pinch	Salt	pinch
4	Large eggs	2

Melt 5 ounces sweet chocolate (2 ounces for 8-inch cake) over simmering water in the top of a double boiler, in a pan over a heat diffuser, or in a microwave oven, and reserve.

In a mixer, whip cream cheese on the highest speed for 5 minutes, then add sugar and beat for 2 minutes more. Add 4/5 of the melted chocolate, espresso, mocha flavoring, rum, and salt and blend together thoroughly. Add the eggs, one at a time, keeping the mixer on the *lowest speed* in order to prevent too much air from destroying the proper consistency of the batter; mix just until each egg has been incorporated into the batter. Chop the ounce of unmelted chocolate into chips and fold into batter. *Or:*

In a food processor, put the sugar in first. Cut each 8-ounce block of cream cheese into eight 1-inch cubes and add the first 8 cubes to bowl. Process using on-off pulse about 25 times, and then add the rest of the cream cheese cubes gradually, blending them in with on-off pulses until mixture is smooth and creamy. When you think it's perfect, blend nonstop for 20 seconds more, then blend in 4/5 of melted chocolate, espresso, mocha flavoring, rum, and salt for 10 seconds. Crack eggs in a bowl, break them up slightly with a fork, add them to batter in processor bowl, and fold them lightly into batter with a rubber spatula to prevent them from sinking to the bottom. Cut the eggs into the batter by using the on-off pulse 10 times, then scrape down the sides with a rubber spatula, and pulse on-off 5 times more. Chop the ounce of unmelted chocolate into chips and fold into batter.

Pour filling into crust and with a knife swirl remaining melted chocolate into batter. Bake in preheated oven.

Baking Time

10″ SPRINGFORM	8″ SPRINGFORM
1 hour + 10 minutes	45 minutes

Remove from oven and let stand on a counter for 10 minutes while you prepare the glaze.

Sour Cream Glaze

10″ SPRINGFORM		8″ SPRINGFORM
2 cups	Sour cream	*1 cup*
¼ cup	Sugar	*2 tablespoons*
1 teaspoon	Light rum	*½ teaspoon*
as needed	Shaved sweet chocolate	*as needed*

Combine sour cream, sugar, and rum with a rubber spatula in a plastic bowl. Spread evenly and smoothly over top of baked filling and return to 350° F oven for 10 minutes. Remove from oven and *immediately* place in refrigerator to cool to prevent cracks from forming in the cake. If desired, shave thin sweet chocolate strips on cake before serving.

For an explanation of how to remove the cake from the springform, see page 19.

MOTHER WONDERFUL'S AMARETTO CHEESECAKE

Preheat oven to 350° F.
Ingredients need not be at room temperature.

Crust

10″ SPRINGFORM		8″ SPRINGFORM
¼ pound (1 stick)	Lightly salted butter	4 tablespoons (½ stick)
2 cups	Finely ground Italian amaretto biscuit crumbs	1 cup + 2 tablespoons
¼ cup	Sugar	2 tablespoons

Melt butter over very low heat. Combine butter with crumbs and sugar in a food processor or with a fork until thoroughly blended. Press small amounts of crust mix all the way up the sides of an ungreased 10-inch springform (2 inches up the sides of an ungreased 8-inch springform) and then press remaining crust mix over bottom of springform. For a more detailed explanation of how to blend and lay down the crust, see pages 17-18.

Filling

10″ SPRINGFORM		8″ SPRINGFORM
2 pounds (four 8-ounce packages)	Cream cheese	1 pound (two 8-ounce packages)
1½ cups	Sugar	¾ cup
1 tablespoon	Amaretto liqueur	1½ teaspoons

10″ SPRINGFORM		8″ SPRINGFORM
1 teaspoon	Vanilla extract	*¹/₂ teaspoon*
1 teaspoon	Almond extract	*¹/₂ teaspoon*
pinch	Salt	*pinch*
4	Large eggs	*2*

In a mixer, whip cream cheese on the highest speed for 5 minutes, then add sugar and beat for 2 minutes more. Add liqueur, extracts, and salt and blend together thoroughly. Add the eggs, one at a time, keeping the mixer on the *lowest speed* in order to prevent too much air from destroying the proper consistency of the batter; mix just until each egg has been incorporated into the batter. *Or:*

If using a food processor, put the sugar in first. Cut each 8-ounce block of cream cheese into eight 1-inch cubes and add the first 8 cubes to bowl. Process using on-off pulse about 25 times, and then add the rest of the cream cheese cubes gradually, blending them in with on-off pulses until mixture is smooth and creamy. When you think it's perfect, blend nonstop for 20 seconds more, then blend in liqueur, extracts, and salt for 5 seconds. Crack eggs in a bowl, break them up slightly with a fork, add them to batter in processor bowl, and fold them lightly into batter with a rubber spatula to prevent them from sinking to the bottom. Cut the eggs into the batter by using the on-off pulse 10 times, then scrape down the sides with a rubber spatula and pulse on-off 5 times more.

Pour batter into crust and bake in preheated oven.

Baking Time

10″ SPRINGFORM	8″ SPRINGFORM
55 minutes	40 minutes

Remove from oven and let stand on a counter for 10 minutes while you prepare the glaze.

Sour Cream Glaze

10″ SPRINGFORM		8″ SPRINGFORM
2 cups	Sour cream	1 cup
¼ cup	Sugar	2 tablespoons
1 teaspoon	Almond extract	½ teaspoon
½ cup	Sliced almonds	¼ cup

Combine sour cream, sugar, and extract with a rubber spatula in a plastic bowl. Spread evenly and smoothly over top of baked filling, sprinkle with almonds, and return to 350° F oven for 10 minutes. Remove from oven and *immediately* place in refrigerator to cool to prevent cracks from forming in the cake.

For an explanation of how to remove the cake from the spring-form, see page 19.

MOTHER WONDERFUL'S GALLIANO CHEESECAKE

Preheat oven to 350° F.
Ingredients need not be at room temperature.

Crust

10″ SPRINGFORM		8″ SPRINGFORM
¼ *pound (1 stick)*	Lightly salted butter	*4 tablespoons (½ stick)*
2 cups	Finely ground arrowroot or tea biscuit crumbs	*1 cup + 2 tablespoons*
¼ *cup*	Sugar	*2 tablespoons*

Melt butter over very low heat. Combine butter with crumbs and sugar in a food processor or with a fork until thoroughly blended. Press small amounts of crust mix all the way up the sides of an ungreased 10-inch springform (2 inches up the sides of an ungreased 8-inch springform) and then press remaining crust mix over bottom of springform. For a more detailed explanation of how to blend and lay down the crust, see pages 17-18.

Filling

10″ SPRINGFORM		8″ SPRINGFORM
2 pounds (four 8-ounce packages)	Cream cheese	1 pound (two 8-ounce packages)
1½ cups	Sugar	¾ cup
½ teaspoon	Almond extract	¼ teaspoon
1 teaspoon	Orange extract	½ teaspoon
4 drops	Anise extract	2 drops
1½ tablespoons	Galliano	2¼ teaspoons
pinch	Salt	pinch
4	Large eggs	2

In a mixer, whip cream cheese on the highest speed for 5 minutes, then add sugar and beat for 2 minutes more. Add extracts, Galliano, and salt and blend thoroughly. Add the eggs, one at a time, keeping the mixer on the *lowest speed* in order to prevent too much air from destroying the proper consistency of the batter; mix just until each egg has been incorporated into the batter. *Or:*

If using a food processor, put the sugar in first. Cut each 8-ounce block of cream cheese into eight 1-inch cubes and add the first 8 cubes to bowl. Process using on-off pulse about 25 times, and then add the rest of the cream cheese cubes gradually, blending them in with on-off pulses until mixture is smooth and creamy. When you think it's perfect, blend nonstop for 20 seconds more, then blend in extracts, Galliano, and salt for 5 seconds. Crack eggs in a bowl, break them up slightly with a fork, add them to batter in processor bowl, and fold them lightly into batter with a rubber spatula to prevent them from sinking to the bottom. Cut the eggs into the batter by using the on-off pulse 10 times, then scrape down the sides with a rubber spatula and pulse on-off 5 times more.

Pour batter into crust and bake in preheated oven.

Baking Time

10″ SPRINGFORM	8″ SPRINGFORM
55 minutes	40 minutes

Remove from oven and let stand on a counter for 10 minutes while you prepare the glaze.

Sour Cream Glaze

10″ SPRINGFORM		8″ SPRINGFORM
2 cups	Sour cream	1 cup
1/4 cup	Sugar	2 tablespoons
1 teaspoon	Almond extract	1/2 teaspoon

Combine sour cream, sugar, and extract with a rubber spatula in a plastic bowl. Spread evenly and smoothly over top of baked filling. Return to 350° F oven for 10 minutes. Remove from oven and *immediately* place in refrigerator to cool to prevent cracks from forming in the cake.

For an explanation of how to remove the cake from the springform, see page 19.

MOTHER WONDERFUL'S
ZABAGLIONE CHEESECAKE

Preheat oven to 350° F.
Ingredients need not be at room temperature.

Crust

10″ SPRINGFORM		8″ SPRINGFORM
¼ pound (1 stick)	Lightly salted butter	4 tablespoons (½ stick)
2 cups	Finely ground Italian wine biscuit crumbs	1 cup + 2 tablespoons
¼ cup	Sugar	2 tablespoons

Melt butter over very low heat. Combine butter with crumbs and sugar in a food processor or with a fork until thoroughly blended. Press small amounts of crust all the way up the sides of an ungreased 10-inch springform (2 inches up the sides of an ungreased 8-inch springform) and then press remaining crust mix over bottom of springform. For a more detailed explanation of how to blend and lay down the crust, see pages 17-18.

Filling

10″ SPRINGFORM		8″ SPRINGFORM
2 pounds (four 8-ounce packages)	Cream cheese	*1 pound (two 8-ounce packages)*
1½ cups	Sugar	*¾ cup*
1 tablespoon	Vov liqueur (my preference) or eggnog flavoring	*1½ teaspoons*
½ teaspoon	Brandy extract	*¼ teaspoon*
1 teaspoon	Marsala	*½ teaspoon*
pinch	Salt	*pinch*
1	Egg yolk	*½*
4	Large eggs	*2*

In a mixer, whip cream cheese on the highest speed for 5 minutes, then add sugar and beat for 2 minutes more. Add liqueur or flavoring, extract, marsala, and salt and blend together thoroughly. Add the yolk and the eggs, one at a time, keeping the mixer on the *lowest speed* in order to prevent too much air from destroying the proper consistency of the batter; mix just until each egg has been incorporated into the batter. *Or:*

If using a food processor, put the sugar in first. Cut each 8-ounce block of cream cheese into eight 1-inch cubes and add the first 8 cubes to bowl. Process using on-off pulse about 25 times, and then add the rest of the cream cheese cubes gradually, blending them in with on-off pulses until mixture is smooth and creamy. When you think it's perfect, blend nonstop for 20 seconds more, then blend in liqueur, extract, marsala, and salt for 5 seconds. Crack yolk and eggs in a bowl, break them up slightly with a fork, add them to batter in processor bowl, and fold them lightly into batter with a rubber spatula to prevent them from sinking to the bottom. Cut the eggs into the batter by using the on-off pulse 10 times, then scrape down the sides with a rubber spatula and pulse on-off 5 times more.

Pour batter into crust and bake in preheated oven.

Baking Time

10″ SPRINGFORM	8″ SPRINGFORM
50 minutes	40 minutes

Remove from oven and let stand on a counter for 10 minutes while you prepare the glaze.

Sour Cream Glaze

10″ SPRINGFORM		8″ SPRINGFORM
2 cups	Sour cream	1 cup
¼ cup	Sugar	2 tablespoons
1 teaspoon	Vov or eggnog flavoring	½ teaspoon

Combine sour cream, sugar, and Vov or flavoring with a rubber spatula in a plastic bowl. Spread evenly and smoothly over top of baked filling and return to 350° F oven for 10 minutes. Remove from oven and *immediately* place in refrigerator to cool to prevent cracks from forming in the cake.

For an explanation of how to remove the cake from the spring-form, see page 19.

MOTHER WONDERFUL'S
MIDDLE EASTERN CHEESECAKE

Preheat oven to 350° F.
Ingredients need not be at room temperature.

Crust

10″ SPRINGFORM		8″ SPRINGFORM
¼ pound (1 stick)	Lightly salted butter	4 tablespoons (½ stick)
1 cup	Finely ground vanilla wafer crumbs	½ cup
1 cup	Finely chopped walnuts	½ cup + 2 tablespoons
¼ cup	Sugar	2 tablespoons

Melt butter over very low heat. Combine butter with crumbs, nuts and sugar in a food processor or with a fork until thoroughly blended. Press small amounts of crust mix all the way up the sides of an ungreased 10-inch springform (2 inches up the sides of an ungreased 8-inch springform) and then press remaining crust mix over bottom of springform. For a more detailed explanation of how to blend and lay down the crust, see pages 17-18.

Filling

10″ SPRINGFORM		8″ SPRINGFORM
2 pounds (four 8-ounce packages)	Cream cheese	1 pound (two 8-ounce packages)
1 1/3 cups	Sugar	2/3 cup
1 teaspoon	Sherry extract	1/2 teaspoon
1 tablespoon	Cream sherry	1 1/2 teaspoons
pinch	Salt	pinch
4	Large eggs	2
6 ounces	Marble halvah	3 ounces

In a mixer, whip cream cheese on the highest speed for 5 minutes, then add sugar and beat for 2 minutes more. Add extract, sherry, and salt and blend together thoroughly. Add the eggs, one at a time, keeping the mixer on the *lowest speed* in order to prevent too much air from destroying the proper consistency of the batter; mix just until each egg has been incorporated into the batter. Chop halvah into 1/4-inch chunks and fold into batter. Or:

If using a food processor, put the sugar in first. Cut each 8-ounce block of cream cheese into eight 1-inch cubes and add the first 8 cubes to bowl. Process using on-off pulse about 25 times, and then add the rest of the cream cheese cubes gradually, blending them in with on-off pulses until mixture is smooth and creamy. When you think it's perfect, blend nonstop for 20 seconds more, then blend in extract, sherry, and salt for 5 seconds. Crack eggs in a bowl, break them up slightly with a fork, add them to batter in processor bowl, and fold them lightly into batter with a rubber spatula to prevent them from sinking to the bottom. Cut the eggs into the batter by using the on-off pulse 10 times, then scrape down the sides with a rubber spatula, and pulse on-off 5 times more. Chop halvah into 1/4-inch chunks and fold into batter with a rubber spatula.

Pour batter into crust and bake in preheated oven.

Baking Time

10″ SPRINGFORM	8″ SPRINGFORM
50 minutes	40 minutes

Remove from oven and let stand on a counter for 10 minutes while you prepare the glaze.

Sour Cream Glaze

10″ SPRINGFORM		8″ SPRINGFORM
2 cups	Sour cream	1 cup
1/4 cup	Sugar	2 tablespoons
1 teaspoon	Cream sherry	1/2 teaspoon
as needed	Chopped halvah	as needed

Combine sour cream, sugar, and sherry with a rubber spatula in a plastic bowl. Spread evenly and smoothly over top of baked filling. Return to 350° F oven for 10 minutes. Remove from oven and *immediately* place in refrigerator to cool to prevent cracks from forming in the cake. Sprinkle with chopped or crushed halvah before serving.

For an explanation of how to remove the cake from the springform, see page 19.

MOTHER WONDERFUL'S
CHESTNUT CHEESECAKE

Preheat oven to 350° F.
Ingredients need not be at room temperature.

Crust

10″ SPRINGFORM		8″ SPRINGFORM
1/4 pound (1 stick)	Lightly salted butter	4 tablespoons (1/2 stick)
2 cups	Finely ground Swedish gingersnap crumbs	1 cup + 2 tablespoons
1/4 cup	Sugar	2 tablespoons

Melt butter over very low heat. Combine butter with crumbs, and sugar in a food processor or with a fork until thoroughly blended. Press small amounts of crust mix all the way up the sides of an ungreased 10-inch springform (2 inches up the sides of an ungreased 8-inch springform) and then press remaining crust mix over bottom of springform. For a more detailed explanation of how to blend and lay down the crust, see pages 17-18.

Filling

10″ SPRINGFORM		8″ SPRINGFORM
1 ounce	Crystallized ginger	1/2 ounce
2 pounds (four 8-ounce packages)	Cream cheese	1 pound (two 8-ounce packages)
1 1/2 cups	Sugar	3/4 cup

10″ SPRINGFORM		8″ SPRINGFORM
½ cup	Unsweetened chestnut purée	¼ cup
1½ tablespoons	Drambuie	2¼ teaspoons
pinch	Salt	pinch
4	Large eggs	2

Slice ginger very thin and reserve.

In a mixer, whip cream cheese on the highest speed for 5 minutes, then add sugar and beat for 2 minutes more. Add purée, Drambuie, ginger, and salt and blend together thoroughly. Add the eggs, one at a time, keeping the mixer on the *lowest speed* in order to prevent too much air from destroying the proper consistency of the batter; mix just until each egg has been incorporated into the batter. *Or:*

If using a food processor, put the sugar in first. Cut each 8-ounce block of cream cheese into eight 1-inch cubes and add the first 8 cubes to bowl. Process using on-off pulse about 25 times, and then add the rest of the cream cheese cubes gradually, blending them in with on-off pulses until mixture is smooth and creamy. When you think it's perfect, blend nonstop for 20 seconds more, then blend in purée, Drambuie, and salt for 5 seconds. Crack eggs in a bowl, break them up slightly with a fork, add them to batter in processor bowl, and fold them lightly into batter with a rubber spatula to prevent them from sinking to the bottom. Cut the eggs into the batter by using the on-off pulse 10 times, then scrape down the sides with a rubber spatula, add ginger and pulse on-off 5 times more.

Pour batter into crust and bake in preheated oven.

Baking Time

10″ SPRINGFORM	8″ SPRINGFORM
55 minutes	40 minutes

Remove from oven and let stand on a counter for 10 minutes while you prepare the glaze.

Sour Cream Glaze

10″ SPRINGFORM		8″ SPRINGFORM
2 cups	Sour cream	1 cup
¼ cup	Sugar	2 tablespoons
1 teaspoon	Drambuie	½ teaspoon
6 drops	Ginger extract	3 drops
1 chunk	Crystallized ginger	1 chunk

Combine sour cream, sugar, Drambuie, and extract with a rubber spatula in a plastic bowl. Spread evenly and smoothly over top of baked filling. Slice ginger into 12 slivers and arrange ginger slices vertically around the rim like numbers on a clockface. Return to 350° F oven for 10 minutes. Remove from oven and *immediately* place in refrigerator to cool to prevent cracks from forming in the cake.

For a more detailed explanation of how to remove the cake from the springform, see page 19.

MOTHER WONDERFUL'S
MINCEMEAT CHEESECAKE

Preheat oven to 350° F.
Ingredients need not be at room temperature.

Crust

10″ SPRINGFORM		8″ SPRINGFORM
¼ *pound (1 stick)*	Lightly salted butter	*4 tablespoons (½ stick)*
2 cups	Finely ground Swedish gingersnap crumbs	*1 cup + 2 tablespoons*
¼ *cup*	Sugar	*2 tablespoons*

Melt butter over very low heat. Combine butter with crumbs, and sugar in a food processor or with a fork until thoroughly blended. Press small amounts of crust mix all the way up the sides of an ungreased 10-inch springform (2 inches up the sides of an ungreased 8-inch springform) and then press remaining crust mix over bottom of springform. For a more detailed explanation of how to blend and lay down the crust, see pages 17-18.

Filling

10″ SPRINGFORM		8″ SPRINGFORM
2 pounds (four 8-ounce packages)	Cream cheese	1 pound (two 8-ounce packages)
1 1/4 cups	Sugar	1/2 cup + 2 tablespoons
1/2 cup	Fresh mincemeat	1/4 cup
1 1/2 tablespoons	Fine cognac	2 1/4 teaspoons
pinch	Salt	pinch
4	Large eggs	2

In a mixer, whip cream cheese on the highest speed for 5 minutes, then add sugar and beat for 2 minutes more. Add mincemeat, cognac, and salt and blend together thoroughly. Add the eggs, one at a time, keeping the mixer on the lowest speed in order to prevent too much air from destroying the proper consistency of the batter; mix just until each egg has been incorporated into the batter. Or:

If using a food processor, put the sugar in first. Cut each 8-ounce block of cream cheese into eight 1-inch cubes and add the first 8 cubes to bowl. Process using on-off pulse about 25 times, and then add the rest of the cream cheese cubes gradually, blending them in with on-off pulses until mixture is smooth and creamy. When you think it's perfect, blend nonstop for 20 seconds more, then blend in mincemeat, cognac and salt for 5 seconds. Crack eggs in a bowl, break them up slightly with a fork, add them to batter in processor bowl, and fold them lightly into batter with a rubber spatula to prevent them from sinking to the bottom. Cut the eggs into the batter by using the on-off pulse 10 times, then scrape down the sides with a rubber spatula, add ginger and pulse on-off 5 times more.

Pour into pan and bake in preheated oven.

Baking Time

10″ SPRINGFORM	8″ SPRINGFORM
55 minutes	40 minutes

Remove from oven and let stand on a counter for 10 minutes while you prepare the glaze.

Sour Cream Glaze

10″ SPRINGFORM		8″ SPRINGFORM
2 cups	Sour cream	1 cup
¼ cup	Sugar	2 tablespoons
1 teaspoon	Cognac	½ teaspoon

Combine sour cream, sugar, and cognac with a rubber spatula in a plastic bowl. Spread evenly and smoothly over top of baked filling. Return to 350° F oven for 10 minutes. Remove from oven and *immediately* place in refrigerator to cool to prevent cracks from forming in the cake.

For an explanation of how to remove the cake from the springform, see page 19.

NEW FLAVOR!

MOTHER WONDERFUL'S
PUMPKIN NUT CHEESECAKE

Preheat oven to 350° F.
Ingredients need not be at room temperature.

Crust

10″ SPRINGFORM		8″ SPRINGFORM
1/4 pound (1 stick)	Lightly salted butter	4 tablespoons (1/2 stick)
1 cup	Finely ground vanilla wafer crumbs	1/2 cup + 2 tablespoons
1 cup	Finely ground spiced wafer crumbs	1/2 cup
1/4 cup	Chopped walnuts	2 tablespoons
1/4 cup	Sugar	2 tablespoons

Melt butter over very low heat. Combine butter with crumbs, nuts, and sugar in a food processor or with a fork until thoroughly blended. Press small amounts of crust mix all the way up the sides of an ungreased 10-inch springform (2 inches up the sides of an ungreased 8-inch springform) and then press remaining crust mix over bottom of springform. For a more detailed explanation of how to blend and lay down the crust, see pages 17-18.

Filling

10″ SPRINGFORM		8″ SPRINGFORM
1½ pounds (three 8-ounce packages)	Cream cheese	12 ounces (one and a half 8-ounce packages)
1¼ cups	Sugar	½ cup + 2 tablespoons
¼ cup	Maple syrup	2 tablespoons
1 cup	Canned pumpkin	½ cup
1 teaspoon	Brandy	½ teaspoon
1½ tablespoons	Irish Mist (my preference), rum, or Drambuie	2¼ teaspoons
1½ teaspoons	Cinnamon	¾ teaspoon
¼ teaspoon	Mace	⅛ teaspoon
⅛ teaspoon	Nutmeg	pinch or two
½ cup	Chopped walnuts	¼ cup
1 ounce	Crystallized ginger, minced	½ ounce
pinch	Salt	pinch
4	Large eggs	2

In a mixer, whip cream cheese on the highest speed for 5 minutes, then add sugar and beat for 2 minutes more. Add maple syrup, pumpkin, brandy, Irish Mist, cinnamon, mace, nutmeg, walnuts, ginger, and salt and blend together thoroughly. Add the eggs, one at a time, keeping the mixer on the *lowest speed* in order to prevent too much air from destroying the proper consistency of the batter; mix just until each egg has been incorporated into the batter. Or:

If using a food processor, put the sugar in first. Cut each 8-ounce block of cream cheese into eight 1-inch cubes and add the first 8 cubes to bowl. Process using on-off pulse about 25 times, and then add the rest of the cream cheese cubes gradually, blending them in with on-off pulses until mixture is smooth and creamy. When you think it's perfect, blend nonstop for 20 seconds more, then blend in syrup, pumpkin, brandy, Irish Mist, cinnamon, mace, nutmeg, walnuts, ginger, and salt for 10 seconds. Crack eggs in a bowl, break them up slightly with a fork, add them to batter in processor bowl, and fold them lightly into batter with a rubber spatula to prevent them from sinking to the bottom. Cut the eggs into the batter by using the on-off pulse 10 times, then scrape down the sides with a rubber spatula, and pulse on-off 5 times more.

Pour batter into crust and bake in preheated oven.

Baking Time

10″ SPRINGFORM	8″ SPRINGFORM
1 hour 10 minutes	45 minutes

Remove from oven and let stand on a counter for 10 minutes, then put it in the refrigerator.

Whipped-Cream Rosettes

10″ SPRINGFORM		8″ SPRINGFORM
1 cup	Heavy cream	1/2 cup
2 tablespoons	Confectioners' sugar	1 tablespoon
2 teaspoons	Cognac	1 teaspoon

About 2 hours before you are ready to serve cheesecake, put beaters and bowl in freezer for 10 minutes to chill. Then whip cream until thick with an electric mixer. Add sugar and cognac and combine until blended. Fit a pastry bag with a star tube, fill with whipped cream, and cover top of cake with rosettes. Return to refrigerator, and cut and serve when ready.

MOTHER WONDERFUL'S
CRANBERRY MINT CHEESECAKE

Preheat oven to 350° F.
Ingredients need not be at room temperature.

Crust

10″ SPRINGFORM		8″ SPRINGFORM
1/4 pound (1 stick)	Lightly salted butter	4 tablespoons (1/2 stick)
2 cups	Finely ground vanilla wafer crumbs	1 cup + 2 tablespoons
1/4 cup	Sugar	2 tablespoons

Melt butter over very low heat. Combine butter with crumbs and sugar in a food processor or with a fork until thoroughly blended. Press small amounts of crumb mix all the way up the sides of an ungreased 10-inch springform (2 inches up the sides of an ungreased 8-inch springform) and then press remaining crumb mix over bottom of springform. For a more detailed explanation of how to blend and lay down the crust, see pages 17-18.

Filling

10″ SPRINGFORM		8″ SPRINGFORM
2 pounds (four 8-ounce packages)	Cream cheese	1 pound (two 8-ounce packages)
1½ cups	Sugar	¾ cup
1½ tablespoons	Mint extract	2¼ teaspoons
pinch	Salt	pinch
4	Large eggs	2
2 cups	Fresh cranberries	1 cup

In a mixer, whip cream cheese on the highest speed for 5 minutes, then add sugar and beat for 2 minutes more. Add mint extract and salt and blend together thoroughly. Add the eggs, one at a time, keeping the mixer on the *lowest speed* in order to prevent too much air from destroying the proper consistency of the batter; mix just until each egg has been incorporated into the batter. Fold in cranberries. *Or:*

If using a food processor, put the sugar in first. Cut each 8-ounce block of cream cheese into eight 1-inch cubes and add the first 8 cubes to bowl. Process using on-off pulse about 25 times, and then add the rest of the cream cheese cubes gradually, blending them in with on-off pulses until mixture is smooth and creamy. When you think it's perfect, blend nonstop for 20 seconds more, then blend in mint extract and salt for 5 seconds. Crack eggs in a bowl, break them up slightly with a fork, add them to batter in processor bowl, and fold them lightly into batter with a rubber spatula to prevent them from sinking to the bottom. Cut the eggs into the batter by using the on-off pulse 10 times, then scrape down the sides with a rubber spatula and pulse on-off 5 times more. Fold in cranberries with a rubber spatula.

Pour batter into crust and bake in preheated oven.

Baking Time

10″ SPRINGFORM	8″ SPRINGFORM
50 minutes	40 minutes

Remove from oven and let stand on a counter for 10 minutes while you prepare the glaze.

Sour Cream Glaze

10″ SPRINGFORM		8″ SPRINGFORM
2 cups	Sour cream	1 cup
1/4 cup	Sugar	2 tablespoons
1 teaspoon	White crème de menthe	1/2 teaspoon

Combine sour cream, sugar, and crème de menthe with a rubber spatula in a plastic bowl. Spread evenly and smoothly over top of baked filling and return to 350° F oven for 10 minutes. Remove from oven and *immediately* place in refrigerator to cool to prevent cracks from forming in the cake.

For an explanation of how to remove the cake from the springform, see page 19.

NEW FLAVOR!

MOTHER WONDERFUL'S
KOSHER FOR PASSOVER CHEESECAKE

Preheat oven to 350°F.
Ingredients need not be at room temperature.

Crust

10″ SPRINGFORM		8″ SPRINGFORM
1/4 pound (1 stick)	Lightly salted butter	4 tablespoons (1/2 stick)
2 cups	Finely ground kosher for Passover chocolate macaroon crumbs	1 cup + 2 tablespoons
1/4 cup	Sugar	2 tablespoons

Melt butter over very low heat. Combine butter with crumbs and sugar in a food processor or with a fork until thoroughly blended. Press small amounts of crumb mix all the way up the sides of an ungreased 10-inch springform (2 inches up the sides of an ungreased 8-inch springform) and then press remaining crumb mix over bottom of springform. For a more detailed explanation of how to blend and lay down the crust, see pages 17-18.

Filling

10″ SPRINGFORM		8″ SPRINGFORM
2 pounds (four 8-ounce packages)	Cream cheese	*1 pound (two 8-ounce packages)*
1 1/2 cups	Sugar	*3/4 cup*
1 1/2 tablespoons	Fresh lemon juice	*2 1/4 teaspoons*
pinch	Salt	*pinch*
4	Large eggs	*2*
1/2 cup	Chopped Brazil nuts	*1/4 cup*

In a mixer, whip cream cheese on the highest speed for 5 minutes, then add sugar and beat for 2 minutes more. Add lemon juice and salt and blend together thoroughly. Add the eggs, one at a time, keeping the mixer on the *lowest speed* in order to prevent too much air from destroying the proper consistency of the batter; mix just until each egg has been incorporated into the batter. Fold in Brazil nuts with a rubber spatula. *Or:*

If using a food processor, put the sugar in first. Cut each 8-ounce block of cream cheese into eight 1-inch cubes and add the first 8 cubes to bowl. Process using on-off pulse about 25 times, and then add the rest of the cream cheese cubes gradually, blending them in with on-off pulses until mixture is smooth and creamy. When you think it's perfect, blend nonstop for 20 seconds more, then blend in lemon juice and salt for 10 seconds. Crack eggs in a bowl, break them up slightly with a fork, add them to batter in processor bowl, and fold them lightly into batter with a rubber spatula to prevent them from sinking to the bottom. Cut the eggs into the batter by using the on-off pulse 10 times, then scrape down the sides with a rubber spatula, and pulse on-off 5 times more. Fold in nuts with a rubber spatula.

Pour batter into crust and bake in preheated oven.

Baking Time

10″ SPRINGFORM	8″ SPRINGFORM
55 minutes	40 minutes

Remove from oven and let stand on a counter for 10 minutes while you prepare the glaze.

Sour Cream Glaze

10″ SPRINGFORM		8″ SPRINGFORM
2 cups	Sour cream	1 cup
1/4 cup	Sugar	2 tablespoons
1 teaspoon	Vanilla extract	1/2 teaspoon
as required	Grated lemon zest	as required
2 tablespoons	Chopped Brazil nuts	1 tablespoon

Combine sour cream, sugar, and vanilla with a rubber spatula in a plastic bowl. Spread evenly and smoothly over top of baked filling, sprinkle nuts around the border, grate lemon zest into the center as decoration, and return to 350° F oven for 10 minutes. Remove from oven and *immediately* place in refrigerator to cool to prevent cracks from forming in the cake.

For an explanation of how to remove the cake from the springform, see page 19.

NOTE: Most of these cheesecakes can be kosher for Passover if you replace whatever crumbs are called for in the crust with a combination of chopped nuts and crumbs from kosher for Passover cookies, and only use liqueurs or flavoring that are also kosher for Passover.

NEW FLAVOR!

MOTHER WONDERFUL'S
PARVE LEMON CHEESECAKE

Preheat oven to 350° F.
Ingredients need not be at room temperature.

Crust

10″ SPRINGFORM		8″ SPRINGFORM
1/4 pound (1 stick)	Margarine	4 tablespoons (1/2 stick)
2 cups	Finely ground crumbs from cookies made with margarine or oil	1 cup + 2 tablespoons
1/4 cup	Sugar	2 tablespoons

Melt margarine over very low heat. Combine margarine with crumbs and sugar in a food processor or with a fork until thoroughly blended. Press small amounts of crumb mix all the way up the sides of an ungreased 10-inch springform (2 inches up the sides of an ungreased 8-inch springform) and then press remaining crumb mix over bottom of springform. For a more detailed explanation of how to blend and lay down the crust, see pages 17-18.

Filling

10″ SPRINGFORM		8″ SPRINGFORM
2 pounds (four 8-ounce packages)	Imitation cream cheese made from tofu	1 pound (two 8-ounce packages)
1³/4 cups	Sugar	³/4 cup + 2 tablespoons
2 tablespoons	Fresh lemon juice	1 tablespoon
pinch	Salt	pinch
4	Large eggs	2

In a mixer, whip imitation cream cheese on the highest speed for 5 minutes, then add sugar and beat for 2 minutes more. Add lemon juice and salt and blend together thoroughly. Add the eggs, one at a time, keeping the mixer on the *lowest speed* in order to prevent too much air from destroying the proper consistency of the batter; mix just until each egg has been incorporated into the batter. *Or:*

Using a food processor, put the sugar and imitation cream cheese in first. The imitation cream cheese I use is soft and always packed in a tub. Blend until mixture is smooth and creamy. Add lemon juice and salt and blend for 5 seconds. Crack eggs in a bowl, break them up slightly with a fork, add them to batter in processor bowl, and fold them lightly into batter with a rubber spatula to prevent them from sinking to the bottom. Cut the eggs into the batter by using the on-off pulse 10 times, then scrape down the sides with a rubber spatula and pulse on-off 5 times more.

Pour batter into crust and bake in preheated oven.

Baking Time

10″ SPRINGFORM	8″ SPRINGFORM
60 minutes	45 minutes

Remove from oven and let stand on a counter for 10 minutes, then place in refrigerator to cool.

This cake does not get a sour cream glaze, because that would make it a dairy product, which could not be eaten after a meat dinner. You could sprinkle this cake with powdered sugar for decoration. Or there are nondairy whipped toppings that could be used, and Margaretin Enterprises (in Long Island) distributes a nondairy sour cream product that could be sweetened, flavored, and used for a glaze. Another possibility for decoration is leftover crumb mix.

Note: You can make a parve cake out of any of the preceding recipes for baked cheesecake, simply by using margarine and parve cookies (or nuts) in the crust, replacing the cream cheese with an equal amount of imitation cream cheese made from tofu, and then baking the filling for 10 minutes more for the 10-inch cheesecake (5 minutes more for the 8-inch cheesecake). Parve cakes still have to sit on the countertop for 10 minutes to solidify, even though they will not have a sour cream glaze.

Unfortunately, the following no-bake cheesecakes cannot be parve, because the no-bake cheesecakes all contain a significant dairy ingredient (sweetened condensed milk) for which there is no non-dairy substitute. *Also, imitation cream cheese made with tofu is not kosher for passover, because it contains bean and corn products, which are not kosher for passover.*

Wise Words about No-Bake Cheesecakes

READ BEFORE MAKING!

I always thought great unbaked cheesecakes were an impossible dream, and for good reason. Most of the recipes I'd seen, including all of the no-bakes in *The Joy of Cheesecake*, were so complicated, I always found it easier to pop one of my regular cakes into the oven.

So how come I undertook no-bakes?

Somebody made me an offer I couldn't refuse. Gary Collins asked me to develop a cheesecake that required no baking for a holiday cooking segment on his "Hour Magazine" show. You don't say no to Gary without giving his request the old school try.

So I put on my thinking cap and went into my kitchen, and when I came out a week later, there were several tasty no-bake cheesecakes in my refrigerator. Gary had only asked for one, but our family motto has always been, "More is better!"

Alvin loved them, but it's hard to credit the raves of a man who eats everything but stewed spleen, so, naturally, I tested these cakes on a more critical audience—a few slightly hostile friends. Even they concurred that these bakeless wonders were creamy and flavorful and tasted as good and often better than many baked cheesecakes they'd eaten.

Gary Collins loved them. So did the hosts of "AM Los Angeles," Philadelphia's "Sunday Side Up," and Manhattan's "Morning Show." My no-bake pumpkin cheesecake even won the heart of that classic curmudgeon Howard Cosell, who told Gary that he'd hated pumpkin until he tasted my instant pumpkin cheesecake.

Everyone was astonished to learn how quickly and easily any one of these no-bake cheesecakes could be whipped up in a food processor, and a record-breaking numbers of viewers called in requesting recipes.

To answer any inquiries, either culinary or philosophical, that might occur to you about this process, we're going to play Twenty Questions . . . or Thirty . . . or Forty. I tend to lack restraint. If you think you've one-upped me and have discovered a question I haven't answered, don't trouble yourself too much. Anything I've omitted isn't worth knowing. Believe me, I measured the ingredients, weighed them, chopped them, whisked them, and mashed them, and when I say something doesn't work, just trust me.

Why Is Melting Chocolate Like Love?

Because, as the song says, you can't hurry it. No matter which method you use, chocolate melts best slowly. If you're using a heat diffuser, keep the burner underneath it on low heat. If you're using a double boiler, the water in the bottom pot should be simmering, not erupting. If you're using a microwave, high power either burns the chocolate or burns the butter. Melt the chocolate alone first on two 20-second segments at a medium low setting. Then add butter and zap butter and partially melted chocolate on medium low for 10 seconds at a time, checking the chocolate after every zap to make sure it doesn't burn. And don't melt the chocolate in the microwave in a teacup. The container in which the chocolate melts should be big enough to hold all the crust ingredients and thus double as a mixing bowl. Adding the other ingredients directly to the melted chocolate and butter assures you of a candy crust with every drop of chocolate to which it is entitled. Incidentally, dark chocolate melts faster and more easily than white chocolate, butterscotch-flavored bits, or peanut butter bits.

How Are Mother Wonderful's
No-Bake Cheesecakes Different from
Most Other No-Bake Cheesecakes?

Most traditional no-bake cheesecakes contain gelatin, an ingredient that always reminds me of childhood afflictions, which Mother treated by giving me squares of gelatin riddled with canned fruit cocktails. Even as a tyke I hated the rubbery appearance and texture of gelatin.

Preparing gelatin is also a pain. It has to be softened in liquid and then dissolved over low heat. Many gelatin-based no-bake cheesecakes also require that you separate eggs and whip up egg whites. Not only does that mean prep work, it means a messy kitchen filled with dirty pans—a double minus, especially if you're pressed for time. Today's cooks have more interesting uses for their spare time than scrubbing pots, and have little interest and/or inclination in keeping their households spotlessly clean. The highest compliment the original Mother Wonderful, my grandmother, ever paid anyone went like this: "Her kitchen was so clean, you could eat off the floor." My mom never uttered a sentence like that in my house. Mom knows floors *that* clean are a relic of the past, and she's lowered her housekeeping standards accordingly. She breathes a sigh of relief when she walks into my kitchen and finds my table clean enough to eat from.

How Do Mother Wonderful's
Unbaked Cheesecakes Prevent Dishpan Hands?

My cakes require *one pan* for melting butter and/or some form of chocolate and *one food processor* for grinding cookies into crumbs and/or chopping nuts and blending batter, *one knife* for cutting whatever needs to be cut, *one fork* for blending the crumb crust, and *one rubber spatula*, which does pretty much anything else—and an optional *whisk*.

How Can I Use a Food Processor
to Make Crusts and Batter
Without Having to Wash It in Between?

Let's start with the crusts. The chocolate and butter are melted together in a double boiler, a microwave oven, a 10-inch frying pan, or a 1½-quart saucepan over a heat diffuser. No matter which method you choose, the pan doubles as your mixing bowl. Just dump all your other crust ingredients into the melted butter/chocolate mixture all at once and combine them by mashing them together with an ordinary fork. That saves you from washing a mixing bowl. Even if you grind your cookie crumbs and nuts from scratch in your food processor, not to worry. They're dry ingredients, and afterward you simply wipe out the bowl of your processor and your blade with a disposable paper towel, and your food processor is ready to cream your cheese.

What if the Filling and Crust Require
Two Different Kinds of Melted Chocolate?

Because the pan you use to melt the chocolate for the crust doubles as a mixing bowl, the dry ingredients will absorb the moisture of the chocolate and butter and leave little or no residue. Just wipe out the pan with a good old paper towel and it's ready to melt whatever different chocolate you'll need for your filling.

What Do You Mean by
Medium-Fine Chopped Nuts?

You really have to watch the nuts when you're chopping them, because if they're too big, they make the crust too chunky, but if they're too fine, they turn into nut butters and make the crust too mushy.

To chop nuts properly for these crusts, process them for 20 seconds and then pulse on-off 15 to 20 times, checking the texture often and stirring the nuts around to see that they are fluffy. Since we want them medium fine, you have to stop chopping before they turn into nut butter. Hard nuts like almonds chop up easily. Softer nuts such as macadamia and pine nuts have to be watched closely or they mush up. If they turn into mush, you can still use them, but next time, if you want the proper texture in your crusts, stop chopping a little bit sooner. Chopping nuts and cookies together in a food processor produces the best results, because the cookie crumbs absorb the excess oils and prevent the nuts from turning mushy.

Why Do Mother Wonderful's Unbaked Crusts Require No Baking?

The crusts are independent and substantial as is. The cohesive element in these unbaked crusts is some form of melted chocolate, which transforms the other ingredients (butter, cookie crumbs, nuts, and flavoring) into a delicious candy shell as it chills.

Why Doesn't This Batter Need to Be Baked?

Acidic juices that come in contact with sweetened condensed milk alter the protein in the milk so that it soaks up liquid. That process sets the batter. The process works best with fresh lime and lemon juice, but other citrus juices will work if their acid content is boosted, which is why I never dilute any of the frozen concentrated juices that are used in these cakes, and why I increase acidity by adding Fruit Fresh to the juices. Fruit Fresh is sweet, otherwise flavorless, and high in ascorbic acid (see note on page 70). The other ingredient that sets batter is melted chocolate, which solidifies when it cools.

What Kind of Pan Works Best for These Cakes?

I really prefer a 10-inch springform for the larger size and an 8-inch springform for the smaller size, because the cakes present better and cut better when they are wide and flat, rather than small and high. The crusts should not go higher than 1½ inches up the sides of the springform. On many of these cakes, 1 inch is sufficient. The lower the sides are, the thicker they can be, and a substantial shell better supports the unbaked batter.

How Should These Cakes Be Served?

Because these particular cakes are rich, sweet confections, small portions (flat, narrow wedges) are really enough for most folks. Gluttons can always request seconds.

Suppose I Don't Have a Springform Pan?

If you're hard-pressed and don't have the correct size of springform, or any springform, use a pie pan, or even a throwaway aluminum pie tin. Please note, however, that pie pans and tins really handle the amount of filling for the 8-inch cake best.

Why Can't I Use a Store-Bought Crumb Crust?

Only if you are at your wits' end would I permit the use of a store-bought crumb crust. Not only do they fail to hold together, I think they taste as if they contain medicated skin cream.

How Long Will These Cakes Take to Set?

Many of these cakes will set after 2 hours of refrigeration, but they are best if they stay in the refrigerator overnight to firm up and intensify their flavors. These no-bake cheesecakes are generally more custardlike than baked cheesecakes, but no-bakes will firm up nicely after two days of refrigeration. As a rule of thumb, the longer the no-bake cheesecakes sit in the refrigerator, the more solid they become, because the chemical process that causes them to set continues to work.

How Long Will They Keep?

They can remain in the refrigerator for a week, I've kept them for two, and they also freeze nicely. The reason they hold up better than baked cheesecakes is that they have no topping, and it's the topping that discolors and makes a cheesecake that's been refrigerated too long look unappetizing.

Do They Have to Be Made on a Metal or Foil-Wrapped Bottom?

I make them in a springform directly on a plain uncovered cardboard round.

Any Other Helpful Hints?

If you find the crust mix very greasy, press it against the sides of the springform with a fork. Otherwise, wrap your fingers in plastic wrap and use your wrapped fingers to press, smooth, and flatten walnut-sized nuggets of crust against the sides. A sheet of plastic wrap will help you press the crust mix over the bottom. If you have any empty spots, cover them with plastic wrap and either run your fingertips or the back of a spoon or your knuckles over the area to spread the crust better.

How Fussy Do I Have to Be about Ingredients?

Because there are no mitigating factors, as in baking, the quality of the flavorings is more important than ever. You can sometimes get away with an artificial extract or flavor when a cake is baked, but for these no-bakes nothing but natural flavors will do. Even the very highest quality artificial flavorings leave a slightly bitter taste.

Avoid the store's brand of cream cheese. I've tested several different supermarkets' own label and they are saltier and more gummy than Kraft's Philadelphia cream cheese. The Philadelphia brand contains some stabilizers like xanthan and/or carob bean and/or guar gums, but they are blended in very acceptable proportions. Another brand I like is Fleur de Lait, an old-fashioned all-natural cream cheese that contains only cultured pasteurized milk and cream and salt and is particularly creamy and tasty.

Is There Any Brand of Sweetened Condensed Milk that's Preferable?

They all taste pretty much alike, so buy the least expensive.

Can I Use a Lower-Calorie Cheese and still Get a Tasty Cake?

There's very little difference between the taste of Kraft's light and their regular cream cheese, and there are 20 fewer calories per ounce (320 less calories per cheesecake). If you want to go "half hog," try the imitation cream cheese that has 40 calories less per ounce (640 fewer calories per cheesecake). That might make a slightly bigger dent, but even if you cut the cake into sixteen slices, you're only getting 20 or 40 calories less per slice—not that much in the grand scheme of weight reduction. But you can use a lower-calorie cheese and still make an instant cheesecake, and I'll show you how in the lower-calorie cheesecake section.

What? No Topping?

As I've said before, bakers designed toppings and icings for the same reasons that chefs designed sauces, to hide a multitude of sins. Cheesecake toppings cover any blemishes in baked cake, like burns, cracks, and carbuncles of undissolved cream cheese. Since the no-bake cheesecakes cannot burn or crack, and since the food processor makes the batter smooth as silk, there's no need for concealment.

You'll see: You can decorate the batter and put the cake in to set and you'll get the very same beautiful pattern on the cake that you designed originally.

What Do I Do with the Other Half-Can of Sweetened Condensed Milk when I Make an 8-Inch Cake that only Requires Half a Can?

Either make a double batch and freeze one cake for next time, or use the remaining condensed milk to make another flavor.

What Do I Do if I Don't Have
the Particular Kind of Nut that's Called
for in a Crust Recipe?

Substitute. I've used different nuts and cookie crumbs to create subtleties in texture and flavor, but these combinations are not gospel. You can always substitute walnuts for any other nut, and use vanilla wafers to replace any other cookie. Just don't blend all-dark chocolate with all-chocolate cookie crumbs. Some may call this blasphemy, but I think it's just too much chocolate in one place at one time.

And you really can replace sweet chocolate with chocolate chips. Since these cakes are last-minute productions, I've tried to restrict the ingredients to items that are found in most supermarkets.

How Should No-Bake Cheesecakes Be Stored?

If the cake will be served within a week, just keep it refrigerated and covered with a cardboard round in the springform pan. If the cake is to be frozen for later use, it can be frozen in the springform as long as the pan is wrapped in aluminum foil. It can also be removed from the springform after it has set and be frozen in a cardboard cake box.

How Long Should the Cakes Sit at
Room Temperature Before Serving?

No more than 15 minutes—just long enough to let the butter in the crust warm a little and release its bond with the metal ring, which allows you to remove the cake from the pan more easily. The no-bakes should be served cold, and can even be cut, served, and eaten frozen.

7

No-Bake Cheesecakes

MOTHER WONDERFUL'S BASIC LIME-ALMOND NO-BAKE CHEESECAKE

Crust

10″ SPRINGFORM		8″ SPRINGFORM
3 tablespoons	Lightly salted butter	1½ tablespoons
4 ounces	White chocolate	2 ounces
¼ teaspoon	Almond extract	⅛ teaspoon
¾ cup	Finely ground vanilla wafer crumbs	½ cup
¾ cup	Almonds, chopped medium fine	½ cup

Melt butter and white chocolate over simmering water in the top of a double boiler, in a saucepan on a heat diffuser, or in a microwave oven. When melted, remove from heat and whisk into a smooth, even mass. Whisk in extract. Measure cookie crumbs into food processor. Add nuts. Process together for 5-second intervals, checking texture frequently. It should be fine and dry, but not mushy. Mash together with a fork until well blended and then deposit in springform. Press and flatten walnut-sized nuggets of crust mix no more than 1½ inches up the sides of the springform pan, wrapping your hand in plastic wrap to give you better control of the mix and to keep it from sticking to your fingers. To spread remainder of crust mix over bottom, press and smooth it down with the back of a soup spoon. The mixture is very malleable and it will really cover the entire bottom. If you still find there are empty spots in the bottom crust, press the side crusts a bit thinner and use the excess to fill in the blanks in the bottom, or just sprinkle some more cookie crumbs around.

Filling

10″ SPRINGFORM		8″ SPRINGFORM
1 pound (two 8-ounce packages)	Cream cheese	½ pound (one 8-ounce package)
1 can (about 1⅓ cups)	Sweetened condensed milk	½ can (about ⅔ cup)
⅓ cup	Fresh lime juice	3 tablespoons
2 tablespoons	Grated lime zest	1 tablespoon

In a mixer, whip cream cheese on highest speed for 5 minutes. Add condensed milk and beat on medium speed for 2 minutes more or until creamy and well blended. Add juice and zest and beat briefly until blended. Or:

In a food processor, whip up cream cheese and condensed milk, using the on-off pulse about 25 times, and then just run the processor for 10 to 15 seconds more or until ingredients are smooth and blended. Add lime juice and zest and process until well blended.

Pour into crust. Spread batter around carefully with a rubber spatula so that it's level and pressed firmly against the crust.

Garnish

Grated lime zest

Sprinkle with grated lime zest and put in refrigerator to set.

To remove cake from springform, let it stand at room temperature for 10-15 minutes to allow the butter to loosen its bond with the metal ring. When you release the springform clasp, the crust will detach from the sides. If any small segments stick to the sides, loosen them by separating the crust from the sides gently with a metal spatula or a sharp knife.

MOTHER WONDERFUL'S NO-BAKE LUSCIOUS LEMON NUT CHEESECAKE

Crust

10″ SPRINGFORM		8″ SPRINGFORM
2 1/2 tablespoons	Lightly salted butter	1 3/4 tablespoons
3 ounces	White chocolate	2 ounces
1/2 teaspoon	Lemon extract	1/4 teaspoon
1 1/2 cups	Blanched almonds, chopped medium fine	1 cup

Melt butter and white chocolate over simmering water in the top of a double boiler, in a saucepan on a heat diffuser, or in a microwave oven. When melted, remove from heat and whisk into a smooth, even mass. Whisk in extract. Measure cookie crumbs into food processor. Add nuts. Process together for 5-second intervals, checking texture frequently. It should be fine and dry, but not mushy. Add crumb/nut mixture all at once to butter mixture. Mash together with a fork until well blended and then deposit in springform. Press and flatten walnut-sized nuggets of crust mix no more than 1½ inches up the sides of the springform pan, and spread remainder over bottom, pressing and smoothing it down with the back of a soup spoon. For a more detailed explanation of how to blend and lay down the crust, see page 158.

Filling

10″ SPRINGFORM		8″ SPRINGFORM
1 pound (two 8-ounce packages)	Cream cheese	½ pound (one 8-ounce package)
1 can (about 1⅓ cups)	Sweetened condensed milk	½ can (about ⅔ cup)
⅓ cup	Fresh lemon juice	2½ tablespoons
¾ teaspoon	Lemon extract	½ teaspoon

In a mixer, whip cream cheese on highest speed for 5 minutes. Add condensed milk and beat on medium speed for 2 minutes more until creamy and well blended. Add juice and extract and beat briefly until blended. Or:

In a food processor, whip up cream cheese and condensed milk, using the on-off pulse 25 times, and then just run the processor for 10 to 15 seconds more, or until ingredients are smooth and blended. Add juice and extract and process until well blended.

Pour into crust. Spread batter around carefully with a rubber spatula so that it's level and pressed firmly against the crust.

Garnish

¼ to ⅓ cup lemon curd or lemon conserve

Dribble lemon conserve around the batter in a circle about 1 inch from the crust and decorate top of cake with it by swirling it around surface with the tip of a knife. Put into refrigerator to set.

For an explanation of how to remove the cake from the springform, see page 159.

MOTHER WONDERFUL'S
NO-BAKE TRIPLE CHOCOLATE CHEESECAKE

Crust

10″ SPRINGFORM		8″ SPRINGFORM
2½ tablespoons	Lightly salted butter	2 tablespoons
2 ounces	Sweet or semisweet chocolate	1½ ounces
1 ounce	White chocolate	1 ounce
½ cup	Finely ground chocolate cookie crumbs	¼ cup
½ cup	Finely ground vanilla wafer crumbs	6 tablespoons
½ cup	Chopped Brazil nuts	6 tablespoons

Melt butter and both chocolates over simmering water in the top of a double boiler, in a saucepan on a heat diffuser, or in a microwave oven. When melted, remove from heat and whisk into a smooth, even mass. Measure cookie crumbs into food processor. Add nuts. Process together for 5-second intervals, checking texture frequently. It should be fine and dry, but not mushy. Add crumb/nut mixture all at once to butter mixture. Mash together with a fork until well blended and then deposit in springform. Press and flatten walnut-sized nuggets of crust mix no more than 1½ inches up the sides of the springform pan, and spread remainder over bottom, pressing and smoothing it down with the back of a soup spoon. For a more detailed explanation of how to blend and lay down the crust, see page 158.

Filling

10″ SPRINGFORM		8″ SPRINGFORM
4 ounces	Dark chocolate, sweet or semisweet	2 ounces
1 pound (two 8-ounce packages)	Cream cheese	1/2 pound (one 8-ounce package)
1 can (about 1 1/3 cups)	Sweetened condensed milk	1/2 can (about 2/3 cup)
2 teaspoons	Fruit Fresh	1 teaspoon
1/3 cup	Frozen orange juice concentrate, undiluted	3 1/2 tablespoons
1 1/2 tablespoon	Fresh lemon juice	2 1/4 teaspoons
1 tablespoon	Grand Marnier	1/2 tablespoon
1/3 cup	Mini-chocolate chips	3 tablespoons

Melt chocolate over simmering water in the top of a double boiler, in a saucepan on a heat diffuser, or in a microwave oven, and reserve.

In a mixer, whip cream cheese on highest speed for 5 minutes. Add condensed milk and beat on medium speed for 2 minutes more or until creamy and well blended. Dissolve Fruit Fresh in juices, add with melted chocolate and Grand Marnier to mixer bowl, and blend well. Or:

In a food processor, whip up cream cheese and condensed milk using the on-off pulse about 25 times, and then just run the processor for 10 to 15 seconds more, or until ingredients are smooth and blended. Dissolve Fruit Fresh in juices, add with melted chocolate and Grand Marnier to processor bowl, and process until well blended.

Fold in mini-chips. Pour into crust. Spread batter around carefully with a rubber spatula so that it's level and pressed firmly against the crust.

Garnish

Any remaining melted chocolate

Pick up any remaining melted chocolate on the point of a knife and decorate top of cake with chocolate swirls. Put cake into refrigerator to set.

For an explanation of how to remove the cake from the spring-form, see page 159.

MOTHER WONDERFUL'S NO-BAKE CHOCOLATE SURPRISE CHEESECAKE

Crust

10″ SPRINGFORM		8″ SPRINGFORM
3 tablespoons	Lightly salted butter	2 tablespoons
4 ounces	Peanut butter bits	3 ounces
3/4 cup	Finely ground chocolate cookie crumbs	1/2 cup
3/4 cup	Peanuts, chopped medium fine	1/2 cup

Melt butter and peanut butter bits over simmering water in the top of a double boiler, in a saucepan on a heat diffuser, or in a microwave oven. When melted, remove from heat and whisk into a smooth, even mass. Measure cookie crumbs into food processor. Add nuts. Process them together for 5-second intervals, checking texture frequently. It should be fine and dry, but not mushy. Add crumb-nut mixture all at once to the butter mixture. Mash together with a fork until well blended and then deposit in springform. Press and flatten walnut-sized nuggets of crust mix no more than 1½ inches up the sides of springform pan, and spread remainder over bottom, pressing and smoothing it down with the back of a soup spoon. For a more detailed explanation of how to blend and lay down the crust, see page 158.

Filling

10″ SPRINGFORM		8″ SPRINGFORM
4 ounces	Peanut butter bits, to be melted	2 ounces
2 ounces	Semisweet chocolate	1 ounce
1 pound (Two 8-ounce packages)	Cream cheese	½ pound (One 8-ounce package)
1 can (about 1⅓ cups)	Sweetened condensed milk	½ can (about ⅔ cup)
2 teaspoons	Fruit Fresh	1 teaspoon
2 tablespoons	Fresh lemon juice	1 tablespoon
¼ cup	Peanut butter bits	2 tablespoons

Melt chocolate and peanut butter bits separately over simmering water in the top of a double boiler, in a saucepan on a heat diffuser, or in a microwave oven, and reserve each.

In a mixer, whip cream cheese on highest speed for 5 minutes. Add condensed milk and beat on medium speed for 2 minutes more, until creamy and well blended. Remove 1 cup of batter (½ cup for 8-inch cake) and reserve. *Or:*

In a food processor, whip up cream cheese and condensed milk using the on-off pulse 25 times, and then just run the processor for 10 to 15 seconds more, or until ingredients are completely smooth and blended. Remove 1 cup of batter (½ cup for 8-inch cake) and reserve.

Add Fruit Fresh dissolved in lemon juice and melted peanut butter bits to batter in processor or mixer and blend well, then fold whole peanut butter bits into this same batter. Pour batter into crust. Spread batter around carefully with a rubber spatula so that it's level and pressed firmly against the crust.

Return reserved plain batter to unwashed processor or mixer bowl and blend melted chocolate in well. Spread this batter evenly over the peanut butter layer with a metal spatula or knife. The top should look as if the cake is solid chocolate, and the peanut butter interior should come as a delightful surprise.

Garnish

Any remaining melted chocolate

Make swirl designs in the top of the cake with any remaining melted chocolate, and refrigerate to set.

For an explanation of how to remove the cake from the springform, see page 159.

MOTHER WONDERFUL'S
NO-BAKE DOUBLEMINT CHEESECAKE

Crust

10″ SPRINGFORM		8″ SPRINGFORM
2 3/4 tablespoons	Lightly salted butter	2 tablespoons
1 ounce	White chocolate	1 ounce
2 ounces	Mint-flavored chocolate or mint-flavored chocolate bits*	1 1/2 ounces
1/4 cup	Finely ground chocolate cookie crumbs	3 tablespoons
1/2 cup	Finely ground vanilla wafer crumbs	5 tablespoons
3/4 cup	Pine nuts, chopped medium fine	1/2 cup

*If you have only plain chocolate or chocolate chips, add 1/2 teaspoon mint extract to crust mix.

Melt butter and both chocolates over simmering water in the top of a double boiler, in a saucepan on a heat diffuser, or in a microwave oven. When melted, remove from heat and whisk into a smooth, even mass. Measure cookie crumbs into food processor bowl. Add nuts. Process together for 5-second intervals, checking texture frequently. It should be fine and dry, but not mushy. Add crumb/nut mixture all at once to butter mixture. Mash together with a fork until well blended and then deposit in springform. Press and flatten walnut-sized nuggets of crust mix no more than 1 1/2 inches up the sides of the springform pan, and spread remainder over bottom, pressing and smoothing it down with the back of a soup spoon. For a more detailed explanation of how to blend and lay down the crust, see page 158.

Filling

10″ SPRINGFORM		8″ SPRINGFORM
4 ounces	Mint-flavored chocolate or mint-flavored chocolate chips	2 ounces
1 pound (two 8-ounce packages	Cream cheese	1/2 pound (one 8-ounce package)
1 can (about 1 1/3 cups)	Sweetened condensed milk	1/2 can (about 2/3 cup)
2 tablespoons + 2 teaspoons	Fruit Fresh	1 tablespoon + 1 teaspoon
2 tablespoons	Fresh lime juice	1 tablespoon
3 tablespoons	White crème de menthe	1 1/2 tablespoons
1 teaspoon	Mint extract	1/2 teaspoon
1/4 cup	Mint-flavored chocolate chips or diced chocolate-covered mint patties	2 tablespoons

Melt chocolate over simmering water in the top of a double boiler, in a saucepan on a heat diffuser, or in a microwave oven, and reserve.

In a mixer, whip cream cheese on highest speed for about 5 minutes. Add condensed milk and beat on medium speed for 2 minutes more until creamy and well blended. Dissolve Fruit Fresh in juice. Add with crème de menthe and extract to mixer bowl and blend well. *Or:*

In a food processor, whip up cream cheese and condensed milk using the on-off pulse 25 times, and then just run the processor for

10 seconds more, or until ingredients are smooth and blended. Dissolve Fruit Fresh in juice, then add to processor bowl with crème de menthe and extract and process until well blended.

Remove 1 cup of batter (½ cup for 8-inch cake), blend melted chocolate into it well, and fold in whole chips or diced mint patties. Pour into crust and spread batter around carefully and evenly so that it's level and pressed firmly against the crust. Cover with the mint-flavored batter. No chocolate should show.

Garnish

Melted chocolate

Sprigs of fresh mint

Pick up any remaining melted chocolate in the pan on the tines of a fork or the point of a knife and decorate top of cake with it by swirling chocolate across surface. Decorate with fresh mint leaves and put into refrigerator to set.

For an explanation of how to remove the cake from the springform, see page 159.

MOTHER WONDERFUL'S
NO-BAKE ESPRESSO SWIRL CHEESECAKE

Crust

10″ SPRINGFORM		8″ SPRINGFORM
3 tablespoons	Lightly salted butter	2 tablespoons
4 ounces	White chocolate	3 tablespoons
2 teaspoons	Instant espresso	1½ teaspoons
1 tablespoon	Strong coffee	2 teaspoons
1 teaspoon	Coffee liqueur	½ teaspoon

10″ SPRINGFORM		8″ SPRINGFORM
½ teaspoon	Coffee extract	*¼ teaspoon*
¾ cup	Finely ground vanilla wafer crumbs	*½ cup*
¾ cup	Walnuts, chopped medium fine	*½ cup*

Melt butter and chocolate over simmering water in the top of a double boiler, in a saucepan on a heat diffuser, or in a microwave oven. When melted, remove from heat and whisk into a smooth, even mass. Dissolve espresso in coffee and whisk in with liqueur and extract. Measure cookie crumbs into food processor. Add nuts. Process together for 5-second intervals, checking texture frequently. It should be fine and dry, but not mushy. Add crumb/nut mixture all at once to butter mixture. Mash together with a fork until well blended and then deposit in springform. Press and flatten walnut-sized nuggets of crust mix no more than 1½ inches up the sides of the springform pan, and spread remainder over bottom, pressing and smoothing it down with the back of a soup spoon.

For a more detailed explanation of how to blend and lay down the crust, see page 158.

Filling

10″ SPRINGFORM		8″ SPRINGFORM
3 ounces	White chocolate	1½ ounces
3 ounces	Sweet chocolate	1½ ounces
1 pound (two 8-ounce packages)	Cream cheese	½ pound (one 8-ounce package)
1 can (about 1⅓ cups)	Sweetened condensed milk	½ can (about ⅔ cup)
4 teaspoons	Fruit Fresh	2 teaspoons
⅓ cup	Frozen orange juice concentrate, undiluted	2½ tablespoons
1 tablespoon	Instant espresso	1½ teaspoons
3 tablespoons	Strong coffee	1½ tablespoons
1½ tablespoons	Coffee extract	2¼ teaspoons
1 tablespoon	Coffee liqueur	1½ teaspoons
⅓ cup (1 ounce)	Mocha-flavored chocolate bar, chopped or cut into chips	2 tablespoons (½ ounce)

Melt white chocolate and sweet chocolate separately and reserve each.

In a mixer, whip cream cheese on highest speed for about 5 minutes. Add condensed milk and beat on medium speed for 2 minutes more until creamy and well blended. Dissolve Fruit Fresh in orange juice. Dissolve instant espresso in coffee, coffee extract, and coffee liqueur and add both mixtures to bowl along with melted white chocolate. Blend well. Or:

In a food processor, whip up cream cheese and condensed milk using the on-off pulse 25 times, and then just run the processor for 10 seconds more, or until ingredients are smooth and blended. Dissolve Fruit Fresh in orange juice. Dissolve instant espresso in coffee, coffee extract, and coffee liqueur and add both mixtures to processor bowl along with melted white chocolate and process until well blended.

Reserve ½ cup of batter (¼ cup for 8-inch cake). Fold mocha-flavored chips into remaining batter and pour into crust. Add melted sweet chocolate to reserved batter and blend well. Pour dark chocolate batter into center of cake and swirl with a rubber spatula to achieve a marbled effect.

Garnish

Mocha-flavored chocolate bar

Chopped walnuts

Use remaining dark chocolate in pan to decorate top. You can also grate mocha-flavored chocolate bar on top or sprinkle on chopped walnuts. Put in refrigerator to set.

For an explanation of how to remove the cake from the spring-form, see page 159.

MOTHER WONDERFUL'S
NO-BAKE BUTTER RUM CORDIAL
CHEESECAKE

Crust

10″ SPRINGFORM		8″ SPRINGFORM
2½ tablespoons	Lightly salted butter	5 teaspoons
5 ounces	Butterscotch bits	3 ounces
1 teaspoon	Dark rum	½ teaspoon + ⅛ teaspoon

10″ SPRINGFORM		8″ SPRINGFORM
3/4 cup	Finely ground vanilla wafer crumbs	*1/2 cup*
3/4 cup	Blanched almonds, chopped medium fine	*1/2 cup*

Melt butter and butterscotch bits over simmering water in the top of a double boiler, in a saucepan on a heat diffuser, or in a microwave oven. When melted, remove from heat and whisk together into a smooth, even mass. Whisk in rum. Measure cookie crumbs into food processor. Add nuts. Process together for 5-second intervals, checking texture frequently. It should be fine and dry, but not mushy. Add crumb/nut mixture all at once to butter mixture. Mash together with a fork until well blended and then deposit in springform. Press and flatten walnut-sized nuggets of crust mix no more than 1½ inches up the sides of the springform pan, and spread remainder over bottom, pressing and smoothing it down with the back of a soup spoon. For a more detailed explanation of how to blend and lay down the crust, see page 158.

Filling

10″ SPRINGFORM		8″ SPRINGFORM
5 *ounces*	Butterscotch bits	3 *ounces*
1 *pound (two 8-ounce packages)*	Cream cheese	½ *pound (one 8-ounce package)*
1 *can (about 1⅓ cups)*	Sweetened condensed milk	½ *can (about ⅔ cup)*
4 *teaspoons*	Fruit Fresh	2 *teaspoons*
¼ *cup*	Dark rum	2 *tablespoons*
2 *tablespoons*	Fresh lemon juice	1 *tablespoon*
2 *tablespoons*	Fresh lime juice	1 *tablespoon*
¼ *cup*	Chopped almonds	2 *tablespoons*
⅓ *cup*	Chocolate-covered rum cordials	¼ *cup*

Melt butterscotch bits over simmering water in the top of a double boiler, in a saucepan on a heat diffuser, or in a microwave oven, and reserve.

In a mixer, whip cream cheese on highest speed for 5 minutes. Add condensed milk and beat on medium speed for 2 minutes more or until creamy and well blended. Dissolve Fruit Fresh in rum and juices, add to mixer bowl with melted butterscotch bits and chopped almonds, and beat briefly until blended. *Or:*

In a food processor, whip up cream cheese and condensed milk using the on-off pulse about 25 times, and then just run the processor for 10 to 15 seconds more, or until ingredients are smooth and blended. Dissolve Fruit Fresh in rum and juices, add to mixer bowl with melted butterscotch bits and chopped almonds, and process for 5 seconds to blend in.

Pour into crust. Spread batter around carefully with a rubber spatula so that it's level and pressed firmly against the crust. Insert the rum cordials into the batter so they do not show and will be a surprise taste treat.

Garnish

Leftover melted butterscotch bits

1 teaspoon dark rum

Whisk rum into any remaining melted butterscotch bits and decorate top of cake with it, by making swirls with the point of a knife. Refrigerate cake to set.

For an explanation of how to remove the cake from the spring-form, see page 159.

MOTHER WONDERFUL'S
NO-BAKE BUTTER BRANDY BRICKLE
CHEESECAKE

Crust

10″ SPRINGFORM		8″ SPRINGFORM
2³/4 tablespoons	Lightly salted butter	1³/4 tablespoons
3 ounces	White chocolate	2 ounces
2 teaspoons	Good brandy	1 teaspoon
³/4 cup	Finely ground shortbread cookie crumbs	¹/2 cup
³/4 cup	Chopped cashews or almonds	¹/2 cup

Melt butter and white chocolate over simmering water in the top of a double boiler, in a saucepan on a heat diffuser, or in a microwave oven. When melted, remove from heat and whisk into a smooth, even mass. Whisk in brandy. Measure cookie crumbs into food pro-cessor. Add nuts. Process together for 5-second intervals, checking texture frequently. It should be fine and dry, but not mushy. Add crumb/nut mixture all at once to butter mixture. Mash together with a fork until well blended, and then deposit in springform. Press and flatten walnut-sized nuggets of crust mix no more than 1½ inches up the sides of the springform pan, and spread remainder over bottom, pressing and smoothing it down with the back of a soup spoon. For a more detailed explanation of how to blend and lay down the crust, see page 158.

Filling

10″ SPRINGFORM		8″ SPRINGFORM
3 ounces	White chocolate	*1½ ounces*
2 ounces	Butterscotch bits	*1 ounce*
1 pound (two 8-ounce packages)	Cream cheese	*½ pound (one 8-ounce package)*
1 can (about 1⅓ cups)	Sweetened condensed milk	*½ can (about ⅔ cup)*
½ teaspoon	Butterscotch extract	*¼ teaspoon*
2 teaspoons	Brandy extract	*1 teaspoon*
2 tablespoons	Good brandy	*1 tablespoon*
2 ounces	Chocolate almond crunch, chopped or cut into ¼-inch dice	*1 ounce*

Melt white chocolate and butterscotch bits together over simmering water in the top of a double boiler, in a saucepan on a heat diffuser, or in a microwave oven, and reserve.

In a mixer, whip cream cheese on highest speed for 5 minutes. Add condensed milk and beat on medium speed for 2 minutes more or until creamy and well blended. Add melted chocolate and butterscotch bits, extracts, and brandy to mixer bowl and beat until blended. *Or:*

In a food processor, whip up cream cheese and condensed milk using the on-off pulse about 25 times, and then just run the processor for 10 to 15 seconds more, or until ingredients are smooth and blended. Add melted chocolate and butterscotch bits, extracts, and brandy to processor bowl and blend well.

Fold in diced crunch. Pour into crust. Spread batter around carefully with a rubber spatula so that it's level and pressed firmly against the crust.

Garnish

Chopped chocolate almond crunch

Sprinkle with crunch and put into refrigerator to set.

For an explanation of how to remove the cake from the springform, see page 159.

MOTHER WONDERFUL'S
NO-BAKE CARAMEL NUT CHEESECAKE

Crust

10″ SPRINGFORM		8″ SPRINGFORM
2½ tablespoons	Lightly salted butter	1¾ tablespoons
3 ounces	White chocolate	2 ounces
¾ teaspoon	Caramel flavoring	½ teaspoon
¾ cup	Finely ground vanilla wafer crumbs	½ cup
¾ cup	Finely chopped pecans	½ cup

Melt butter and white chocolate over simmering water in the top of a double boiler, in a saucepan on a heat diffuser, or in a microwave oven. When melted, remove from heat and whisk into a smooth, even mass. Whisk in caramel flavoring. Measure cookie crumbs into food processor. Add nuts. Process together for 5-second intervals, checking texture frequently. It should be fine and dry, but not mushy. Add crumb/nut mixture all at once to butter mixture. Mash together with a fork until well blended and then deposit in springform. Press and flatten walnut-sized nuggets of crust mix no more than 1 1/2 inches up the sides of the springform pan, and spread remainder over bottom, pressing and smoothing it down with the back of a soup spoon. For a more detailed explanation of how to blend and lay down the crust, see page 158.

Filling

10″ SPRINGFORM		8″ SPRINGFORM
5 *ounces*	White chocolate	2 1/2 *ounces*
1 *pound (two 8-ounce packages)*	Cream cheese	1/2 *pound (one 8-ounce package)*
1 *can (about 1 1/3 cups)*	Sweetened condensed milk	1/2 *can (about 2/3 cup)*
2 *teaspoons*	Fruit Fresh	1 *teaspoon*
1 *tablespoon*	Fresh lemon juice	1 1/2 *teaspoons*
1 *teaspoon*	Caramel flavoring	1/2 *teaspoon*

Melt white chocolate over simmering water in the top of a double boiler, in a saucepan on a heat diffuser, or in a microwave oven, and reserve.

In a mixer, whip cream cheese on highest speed for 5 minutes. Add condensed milk and beat on medium speed for 2 minutes more, or until creamy and well blended. Dissolve Fruit Fresh in juice, add with melted chocolate and caramel flavoring to mixer bowl, and beat briefly until blended. *Or:*

In a food processor, whip up cream cheese and condensed milk using the on-off pulse about 25 times, and then just run the processor for 10 to 15 seconds more, or until ingredients are smooth and blended. Dissolve Fruit Fresh in juice, add with melted chocolate and caramel flavoring to processor bowl, and blend well.

Pour into crust. Spread batter around carefully with a rubber spatula so that it's level and pressed firmly against the crust.

Garnish

1/2 cup chopped pecans

1/4 cup caramel-flavored topping

Sprinkle pecans on cake. Drizzle topping around them and then swirl in with a fork or the point of a knife to make a attractive pattern on the top of the cake. Put into refrigerator to set.

For an explanation of how to remove the cake from the springform, see page 159.

MOTHER WONDERFUL'S NO-BAKE TROPICAL FRUIT CHEESECAKE

Crust

10″ SPRINGFORM		8″ SPRINGFORM
2 3/4 tablespoons	Lightly salted butter	1 3/4 tablespoons
3 ounces	White chocolate	2 ounces
1 teaspoon	Coconut extract	3/4 teaspoon
3/4 cup	Finely ground vanilla wafer crumbs	1/2 cup
6 tablespoons (1/4 cup + 2 tablespoons)	Almonds, chopped medium fine	1/4 cup
2 tablespoons	Grated coconut	2 tablespoons
1/4 cup (1 1/2 ounces)	Dried papaya	3 tablespoons

Melt butter and white chocolate over simmering water in the top of a double boiler, in a saucepan on a heat diffuser, or in a microwave oven. When melted, remove from heat and whisk into a smooth, even mass. Whisk in extract. Measure cookie crumbs into food processor. Add nuts, coconut, and papaya. Process together for 5-second intervals, checking texture frequently. It should be fine and dry, but not mushy. Add crumb/nut mixture all at once to butter mixture. Mash together with a fork until well blended and then deposit in springform. Press and flatten walnut-sized nuggets of crust mix no more than 1½ inches up the sides of the springform pan, and spread remainder over bottom, pressing and smoothing it down with the back of a soup spoon. For a more detailed explanation of how to blend and lay down the crust, see page 158.

Filling

10″ SPRINGFORM		8″ SPRINGFORM
1 ounce	Dried papaya	½ ounce
1 tablespoon	Light rum	1½ teaspoons
1 pound (two 8-ounce packages)	Cream cheese	½ pound (one 8-ounce package)
1 can (about 1⅓ cups)	Sweetened condensed milk	½ can (about ⅔ cup)
4 teaspoons	Fruit Fresh	2 teaspoons
1 tablespoon	Fresh lime juice	1½ teaspoons
1 tablespoon	Fresh lemon juice	1½ teaspoons
⅓ cup	Frozen tropical juice concentrate that contains guava or passion fruit, undiluted*	3 tablespoons
2 teaspoons	Guava extract	1 teaspoon

*Both Welch and Dole make one.

Slice dried papaya very thin, soak in rum, and reserve.

In a mixer, whip cream cheese on highest speed for 5 minutes. Add condensed milk and beat on medium speed for 2 minutes more, or until creamy and well blended. Dissolve Fruit Fresh in juices and guava extract, add to mixer bowl, and blend well. *Or:*

In a food processor, whip cream cheese and condensed milk using the on-off pulse about 25 times, and then just run the processor for 10 to 15 seconds more, or until ingredients are smooth and blended. Dissolve Fruit Fresh in juices and guava extract, add to processor bowl, and blend in well.

Fold in dried papaya and rum. Pour into crust. Spread batter around carefully with a rubber spatula so that it's level and pressed firmly against the crust.

Garnish

Thin slices of dried papaya

Grated coconut

Decorate with thin slices of dried papaya and/or sprinkle with grated coconut. Place cake in refrigerator to set.

For a more detailed explanation of how to remove the cake from the springform, see page 159.

MOTHER WONDERFUL'S
NO-BAKE COCOMANGO
CHEESECAKE

Crust

10″ SPRINGFORM		8″ SPRINGFORM
2¾ tablespoons	Lightly salted butter	1½ tablespoons
5 ounces	White chocolate	3 ounces
1 teaspoon	Coconut extract	½ teaspoon
¾ cup	Finely ground vanilla wafer crumbs	½ cup
¾ cup	Chopped macadamia nuts	½ cup

Melt butter and white chocolate over simmering water in the top of a double boiler, in a saucepan on a heat diffuser, or in a microwave oven. When melted, remove from heat and whisk into a smooth, even mass. Whisk in extract. Measure cookie crumbs into food processor. Add nuts. Process together for 5-second intervals, checking texture frequently. It should be fine and dry, but not mushy. Add crumb-nut mixture all at once to butter mixture. Mash together with a fork until well blended and then deposit in springform. Press and flatten walnut-sized nuggets of crust mix no more than 1½ inches up the sides of the springform pan, and spread remainder over bottom, pressing and smoothing it down with the back of a soup spoon. For a more detailed explanation of how to blend and lay down the crust, see page 158.

Filling

10″ SPRINGFORM		8″ SPRINGFORM
4 ounces	White chocolate	2 ounces
1 pound (two 8-ounce packages)	Cream cheese	1/2 pound (one 8-ounce package)
1 can (about 1 1/3 cups)	Sweetened condensed milk	1/2 can (about 2/3 cup)
2 tablespoons	Fruit Fresh	1 tablespoon
1/3 cup	Pineapple-orange juice frozen concentrate, undiluted	2 1/2 tablespoons
3 tablespoons	Mango extract	1 1/2 tablespoons
1 tablespoon	Anisette	1 1/2 teaspoons
1 cup	Chopped fresh ripe mango	1/2 cup

Melt white chocolate over simmering water in the top of a double boiler, in a saucepan on a heat diffuser or in a microwave oven, and reserve.

In a mixer, whip cream cheese on highest speed for 5 minutes. Add condensed milk and beat on medium speed for 2 minutes more, until creamy and well blended. Dissolve Fruit Fresh in juice. Add to cream cheese along with melted white chocolate, extract, and anisette. Beat briefly until blended. Or:

In a food processor, whip up cream cheese and condensed milk using the on-off pulse 25 times, and then just run the processor for 10 seconds more, or until ingredients are smooth and blended. Dissolve Fruit Fresh in juice, add to cream cheese along with white chocolate, extract, and anisette and process until well blended.

Fold in mango. Pour into crust and spread batter around carefully and evenly so that it's level and pressed firmly against the crust.

Garnish

⅓ cup grated coconut

Sprinkle with coconut and put cake into refrigerator to set.

MOTHER WONDERFUL'S NO-BAKE
PIÑA COLADA CHEESECAKE

Crust

10″ SPRINGFORM		8″ SPRINGFORM
2½ tablespoons	Lightly salted butter	1½ tablespoons
3 ounces	White chocolate	2 ounces
½ cup	Finely ground vanilla wafer crumbs	5 tablespoons
¾ cup	Grated coconut	½ cup
½ cup	Chopped almonds	5 tablespoons

Melt butter and chocolate over simmering water in the top of a double boiler, in a saucepan on a heat diffuser, or in a microwave oven. When melted, remove from heat and whisk into a smooth, even mass. Measure cookie crumbs into food processor. Add coconut and nuts. Process together for 5-second intervals, checking texture frequently. It should be fine and dry, but not mushy. Add crumb/coconut/nut mixture all at once to butter mixture. Mash together with a fork until well blended and then deposit in springform. Press and flatten walnut-sized nuggets of crust mix no more than 1½ inches up the sides of the springform pan, and spread remainder over bottom, pressing and smoothing it down with the back of a soup spoon. For a more detailed explanation of how to blend and lay down the crust, see page 158.

Filling

10″ SPRINGFORM		8″ SPRINGFORM
2 rounds	Dried pineapple	1 round
2 tablespoons	Dark rum	1 tablespoon
1 pound (two 8-ounce packages)	Cream cheese	1/2 pound (one 8-ounce package)
1 can (about 1 1/3 cups)	Sweetened condensed milk	1/2 can (about 2/3 cup)
2 teaspoons	Fruit Fresh	1 teaspoon
1/3 cup	Frozen pineapple juice concentrate, undiluted	2 1/2 tablespoons
2 tablespoons	Fresh lime juice	1 tablespoon
1 teaspoon	Coconut extract	1/2 teaspoon
1/4 cup	Grated coconut	2 tablespoons

Slice pineapple into very thin slices and soak in rum.

Melt butter and chocolate over simmering water in the top of a double boiler, in a saucepan on a heat diffuser, or in a microwave oven, and reserve.

In a mixer, whip cream cheese on highest speed for 5 minutes. Add condensed milk and beat on medium speed for 2 minutes more, until creamy and well blended. Dissolve Fruit Fresh in juices. Add, with extract, and beat briefly until blended. *Or:*

In a food processor, whip up cream cheese and condensed milk using the on-off pulse 25 times, and then just run the processor for 10 seconds more, or until ingredients are smooth and blended. Dissolve Fruit Fresh in juices, add to cream cheese in processor bowl along with extract. Process until well blended.

Fold in coconut, soaked pineapple, and rum. Pour into crust and spread batter around carefully and evenly so that it's level and pressed firmly against the crust.

Garnish

Grated coconut

Sprinkle cake with a handful of coconut and put in refrigerator to set.

For an explanation of how to remove the cake from the spring-form, see page 159.

MOTHER WONDERFUL'S
NO-BAKE CARIBBEAN BANANA CHEESECAKE

Crust

10″ SPRINGFORM		8″ SPRINGFORM
2³/4 *tablespoons*	Lightly salted butter	2 *tablespoons*
5 *ounces*	White chocolate	3 *ounces*
1/2 *teaspoon*	Banana flavoring	1/2 *teaspoon*
3/4 *cup*	Finely ground vanilla wafer crumbs	1/2 *cup*
1/4 *cup*	Banana chips, chopped	3 *tablespoons*
1/2 *cup*	Pecans, chopped medium fine	5 *tablespoons*

Melt butter and chocolate over simmering water in the top of a double boiler, in a saucepan on a heat diffuser, or in a microwave oven. When melted, remove from heat and whisk into a smooth, even mass. Whisk in banana flavoring. Measure cookie crumbs into food processor. Add banana chips and nuts. Process together for 5-second intervals, checking texture frequently. It should be fine and dry, but not mushy. Add crumb/nut mixture all at once to butter mixture. Mash together with a fork until well blended and then deposit in springform. Press and flatten walnut-sized nuggets of crust mix no more than 1½ inches up the sides of the springform pan, and spread remainder over bottom, pressing and smoothing it down with the back of a soup spoon.

OPTIONAL: Reserve two tablespoons of crust to sprinkle on completed cake.

For a more detailed explanation of how to blend and lay down the crust, see page 158.

Filling

10″ SPRINGFORM		8″ SPRINGFORM
3 ounces	White chocolate	1½ ounces
1 pound (two 8-ounce packages)	Cream cheese	½ pound (one 8-ounce package)
1 can (about 1⅓ cups)	Sweetened condensed milk	½ can (about ⅔ cup)
4 teaspoons	Fruit Fresh	2 teaspoons
⅓ cup	Frozen pineapple-orange-banana juice concentrate, undiluted	2½ tablespoons
2 tablespoons	Fresh lime juice	1 tablespoon
2 tablespoons	Fresh lemon juice	1 tablespoon
½ teaspoon	Banana flavoring	¼ teaspoon
2 teaspoons	Dark rum	1 teaspoon

10″ SPRINGFORM		8″ SPRINGFORM
1 ½ *peeled (about 6 ounces)*	Very ripe banana, mashed	¾ *peeled (about 3 ounces)*
½	Banana, sliced thin	¼

Melt butter and white chocolate over simmering water in the top of a double boiler, in a saucepan on a heat diffuser, or in a microwave oven, and reserve.

In a mixer, whip cream cheese on highest speed for 5 minutes. Add condensed milk and beat on medium speed for 2 minutes more, until creamy and well blended. Dissolve Fruit Fresh in juices. Add to cream cheese along with flavoring, rum, melted chocolate, and mashed banana. Beat briefly until blended. *Or:*

In a food processor, whip up cream cheese and condensed milk using the on-off pulse 25 times, and then just run the processor for 10 seconds more or until ingredients are smooth and blended. Dissolve Fruit Fresh in juices, add to cream cheese along with flavorings, rum, melted chocolate, and mashed banana. Process until well blended.

Fold in sliced banana. Pour into crust and spread batter around carefully and evenly so that it's level and pressed firmly against the crust.

Suggested Garnishes

10 whole banana chips and

1 tablespoon chopped walnuts

Chopped banana chips

Reserved crust mixture

Insert banana chips so they stick up out of the batter in a clock pattern and sprinkle with chopped walnuts, or just sprinkle with chopped banana chips or crust mix and put into refrigerator to set.

For an explanation of how to remove the cake from the springform, see page 159.

MOTHER WONDERFUL'S NO-BAKE BANANA SPLIT CHEESECAKE

Crust

10″ SPRINGFORM		8″ SPRINGFORM
2¾ tablespoons	Lightly salted butter	2 tablespoons
3 ounces	Semisweet or sweet chocolate	2 ounces
½ cup	Finely ground chocolate cookie crumbs	6 tablespoons
¼ cup	Finely ground vanilla wafer crumbs	3 tablespoons
½ cup	Walnuts, chopped medium fine	6 tablespoons

Melt butter and chocolate over simmering water in the top of a double boiler, in a saucepan on a heat diffuser, or in a microwave oven. When melted, removed from heat and whisk into a smooth, even mass. Measure cookie crumbs into food processor. Add nuts. Process together for 5-second intervals, checking texture frequently. It should be fine and dry, but not mushy. Add crumb-nut mixture all at once to butter mixture. Mash together with a fork until well blended and then deposit in springform. Press and flatten walnut-sized nuggets of crust mix no more than 1½ inches up the sides of the springform pan, and spread remainder over bottom, pressing and smoothing it down with the back of a soup spoon.

For a more detailed explanation of how to blend and lay down the crust, see page 158.

Filling

10″ SPRINGFORM		8″ SPRINGFORM
2 ounces	Dark chocolate, sweet or semisweet	1 ounce
1 pound (two 8-ounce packages)	Cream cheese	½ pound (one 8-ounce package)
1 can (about 1⅓ cups)	Sweetened condensed milk	½ can (about ⅔ cup)
4 teaspoons	Fruit Fresh	2 teaspoons
⅓ cup	Frozen pineapple-orange-banana juice concentrate, undiluted	2½ tablespoons
2 tablespoons	Fresh lime juice	1 tablespoon
2 tablespoons	Fresh lemon juice	1 tablespoon
½ teaspoon	Banana flavoring	¼ teaspoon
1 whole peeled (about 4 ounces)	Very ripe banana, mashed	½ peeled (2 ounces)
1 whole	Ripe banana, sliced thin	½
¼ cup	"Wet" nuts (from walnut dessert topping), drained and chopped	2 tablespoons

Melt chocolate over simmering water in the top of a double boiler, in a saucepan on a heat diffuser, or in a microwave, and reserve.

In a mixer, whip cream cheese on highest speed for 5 minutes. Add condensed milk and beat on medium speed for 2 minutes more, until creamy and well blended. Remove 1 cup of batter (½ cup for 8-inch cake), add melted chocolate to it, and reserve. Dissolve

Fruit Fresh in juices and add to remaining cream cheese in mixer bowl along with flavoring and mashed banana. Beat briefly until blended. *Or:*

In a food processor, whip up cream cheese and condensed milk using the on-off pulse 25 times, and then just run the processor for 10 seconds more, or until ingredients are smooth and blended. Remove 1 cup of batter, add melted chocolate to it, and reserve. Dissolve Fruit Fresh in juices and add to cream cheese in processor bowl along with flavoring and mashed banana. Process until well blended.

Fold in sliced banana and nuts. Pour into crust and spread batter around carefully and evenly so that it's level and pressed firmly against the crust. Add chocolate batter to middle and swirl with a rubber spatula to achieve a marbled effect. Put into refrigerator to set.

Garnish

Hot fudge sauce

Whipped cream

Maraschino cherries

Right before serving, dribble a spoonful of hot fudge sauce on each slice and top with a dollop of whipped cream and one maraschino cherry, just like a sundae or banana split.

For an explanation of how to remove the cake from the springform, see page 159.

MOTHER WONDERFUL'S
NO-BAKE BERRY MINT CHEESECAKE

Crust

10″ SPRINGFORM		8″ SPRINGFORM
2¾ tablespoons	Lightly salted butter	2 tablespoons
3 ounces	White chocolate	2 ounces
½ teaspoon	Mint extract	¼ teaspoon
1 cup	Finely ground vanilla wafer or tea biscuit crumbs	½ cup + 2 tablespoons
½ cup	Pine nuts, chopped medium fine	⅓ cup

Melt butter and white chocolate over simmering water in the top of a double boiler, in a saucepan on a heat diffuser, or in a microwave oven. When melted, remove from heat and whisk into a smooth, even mass. Whisk in extract. Measure cookie crumbs into food processor. Add nuts. Process together for 5-second intervals, checking texture frequently. It should be find and dry, but not mushy. Add crumb/nut mixture all at once to butter mixture. Mash together with a fork until well blended and then deposit in springform. Press and flatten walnut-sized nuggets of crust mix no more than 1½ inches up the sides of the springform pan, and spread remainder over bottom, pressing and smoothing it down with the back of a soup spoon.

For a more detailed explanation of how to blend and lay down the crust, see page 158.

NOTE: This happens to be a very elegant crust. The pine nuts are particularly nice to work with, because they are crunchy yet rather bland. Make a double batch of this crust and put it in the freezer for an emergency when you have to put a pie together quickly and you don't have lots of time to fuss. Then you can just zap the frozen crust in the microwave to heat it up and make it malleable, and proceed.

Filling

10″ SPRINGFORM		8″ SPRINGFORM
1 pound (two 8- ounce packages)	Cream cheese	1/2 pound (one 8- ounce package)
1 can (about 1 1/3 cups)	Sweetened condensed milk	1/2 can (about 2/3 cup)
2 1/2 tablespoons	Fresh lemon juice	1 tablespoon + 1 teaspoon
3 tablespoons	Fresh lime juice	1 1/2 tablespoons
1 tablespoon	White crème de menthe	1 1/2 teaspoons
1 teaspoon	Spearmint extract	1/2 teaspoon
2 cups	Fresh blueberries, raspberries, or blackberries (not strawberries; they're too ordinary for this elegant batter)	1 cup

In a mixer, whip cream cheese on highest speed for 5 minutes. Add condensed milk and beat on medium speed for 2 minutes more, or until creamy and well blended. Add juices, crème de menthe, and extract to mixer bowl, and beat briefly until blended. Or:

In a food processor, whip up cream cheese and condensed milk using the on-off pulse about 25 times, and then just run the processor for 10 to 15 seconds more or until ingredients are smooth and blended. Add juices, crème de menthe, and extract to mixer bowl and beat briefly until blended.

Fold in berries very gently with a rubber spatula, so they don't break, and pour batter into crust. Spread batter around carefully with a rubber spatula so that it's level and pressed firmly against the crust.

Garnish

Berries

Fresh mint leaves

Decorate with a few more berries and some artfully placed fresh mint leaves. Place in refrigerator to set.

For an explanation of how to remove the cake from the spring-form, see page 159.

MOTHER WONDERFUL'S NO-BAKE MANDARIN ORANGE CHEESECAKE

Crust

10″ SPRINGFORM		8″ SPRINGFORM
2 1/2 *tablespoons*	Lightly salted butter	1 1/2 *tablespoons*
5 *ounces*	White chocolate	3 *ounces*
2 *teaspoons*	Grand Marnier	1 *teaspoon*
3/4 *cup*	Finely ground shortbread cookie crumbs	1/2 *cup*
3/4 *cup*	Almonds, chopped medium fine	1/2 *cup*

Melt butter and white chocolate over simmering water in the top of a double boiler, in a saucepan on a heat diffuser, or in a microwave oven. When melted, remove from heat and whisk into a smooth, even mass. Whisk in Grand Marnier. Measure cookie crumbs into food processor. Add nuts. Process together for 5-second intervals, checking texture frequently. It should be fine and dry, but not mushy. Add together with a fork until well blended and then deposit in springform. Press and flatten walnut-sized nuggets of crust mix no more than 1½ inches up the sides of the springform pan, and spread remainder over bottom, pressing up and smoothing it down with the back of a soup spoon. For a more detailed explanation of how to blend and lay down the crust, see page 158.

Filling

10″ SPRINGFORM		8″ SPRINGFORM
5 ounces	White chocolate	3 ounces
One 14-ounce can	Mandarin oranges	One 11-ounce can
1 pound (two 8-ounce packages)	Cream cheese	½ pound (one 8-ounce package)
1 can (about 1⅓ cups)	Sweetened condensed milk	½ can (about ⅔ cup)
4 teaspoons	Fruit Fresh	2 teaspoons
⅓ cup	Frozen orange juice, undiluted	2½ tablespoons
2 tablespoons	Fresh lemon juice	1 tablespoon
1½ tablespoons	Grand Marnier	2¼ teaspoons
¾ teaspoon	Almond extract	¼ teaspoon + ⅛ teaspoon

Melt white chocolate over simmering water in the top of a double boiler, in a saucepan on a heat diffuser, or in a microwave oven, and reserve.

Drain orange segments, discard syrup, and blot orange segments well on paper towels. Reserve the 12 most attractive segments for the decorative topping.

In a mixer, whip cream cheese on highest speed for 5 minutes. Add condensed milk and beat on medium speed for 2 minutes more, or until creamy and well blended. Dissolve Fruit Fresh in combined juices, add to mixer bowl with Grand Marnier, extract, and the least attractive orange segments and blend well. *Or:*

In a food processor, whip up cream cheese and condensed milk using the on-off pulse 25 times, and then just run the processor for 10 to 15 second more, or until the ingredients are smooth and blended. Dissolve Fruit Fresh in combined juices, add to processor bowl with Grand Marnier, extract, and least attractive orange segments. Blend for 5 seconds. The oranges should disintegrate.

Pour batter into crust and spread batter around carefully with a rubber spatula so that it's level and pressed firmly against the crust.

Garnish

12 well-drained canned mandarin orange segments

Arrange segments on top like the numbers on a clock face, and put cake into refrigerator to set.

For an explanation of how to remove the cake from the springform, see page 159.

MOTHER WONDERFUL'S
NO-BAKE FRAMBOISE CHEESECAKE

Crust

10″ SPRINGFORM		8″ SPRINGFORM
3 tablespoons	Lightly salted butter	2 tablespoons
4 ounces	White chocolate	3 ounces
3/4 cup	Finely ground vanilla wafer crumbs	1/2 cup
3/4 cup	Pine nuts, chopped medium fine	1/2 cup

Melt butter and chocolate over simmering water in the top of a double boiler, in a saucepan on a heat diffuser, or in a microwave oven. When melted, remove from heat and whisk into a smooth, even mass. Measure cookie crumbs into food processor. Add nuts. Process together for 5-second intervals, checking texture frequently. It should be fine and dry, but not mushy. Add crumb/nut mixture all at once to butter mixture. Mash together with a fork until well blended and then deposit in springform. Press and flatten walnut-sized nuggets of crust mix no more than 1½ inches up the sides of the springform pan, and spread remainder over bottom, pressing and smoothing it down with the back of a soup spoon. For a more detailed explanation of how to blend and lay down the crust, see page 158.

Filling

10″ SPRINGFORM		8″ SPRINGFORM
5 ounces	White chocolate	2 ½ ounces
1 pound (two 8-ounce packages)	Cream cheese	½ pound (one 8-ounce package)
1 can (about 1⅓ cups)	Sweetened condensed milk	½ can (about ⅔ cup)
2 teaspoons	Fruit Fresh	1 teaspoon
1 tablespoon	Lemon juice	1 ½ teaspoons
3 tablespoons	Framboise (raspberry brandy)	1 ½ tablespoons
1 cup	Fresh or frozen raspberries	½ cup

Melt chocolate over simmering water in the top of a double boiler, in a saucepan on a heat diffuser, or in a microwave oven, and reserve.

In a mixer, whip cream cheese on highest speed for 5 minutes. Add condensed milk and beat on medium speed for 2 minutes more, or until creamy and well blended. Dissolve Fruit Fresh in lemon juice. Add with melted chocolate and framboise to mixer bowl and blend well. *Or:*

In a food processor, whip cream cheese and condensed milk using the on-off pulse about 25 times, and then just run the processor for 10 to 15 seconds more, or until ingredients are smooth and blended. Dissolve Fruit Fresh in lemon juice. Add with melted chocolate and framboise to processor bowl and blend well.

Fold in raspberries, taking care not to smash them. Pour into crust. Spread batter around carefully with a rubber spatula so that it's level and pressed firmly against the crust.

Garnish

Fresh raspberries

Pick up any remaining melted white chocolate in the pan on the tines of a fork or the point of a knife and decorate the top of cake with it, by swirling chocolate across top surface. Put into refrigerator to set. Place raspberries in an attractive pattern on top.

For an explanation of how to remove the cake from the spring-form, see page 159.

MOTHER WONDERFUL'S
NO-BAKE RASPBERRY RHUBARB
CHEESECAKE

Preliminary

10″ SPRINGFORM		8″ SPRINGFORM
1 pound	Frozen rhubarb	1/2 pound
1/4 cup	Water	2 tablespoons
3/4 cup	Sugar	6 tablespoons

Boil rhubarb and water together for 5 minutes, then add sugar and simmer, covered, for 20 minutes more. During this time you can make your crust and prepare most of your batter. When rhubarb is finished, drain, discard juice, and reserve rhubarb pieces.

Crust

10″ SPRINGFORM		8″ SPRINGFORM
2³/4 tablespoons	Lightly salted butter	1³/4 tablespoons
3 ounces	White chocolate	2 ounces
1 teaspoon	Raspberry extract	³/4 teaspoon
³/4 cup	Finely ground tea biscuit or vanilla wafer crumbs	¹/2 cup
³/4 cup	Chopped pine nuts	¹/2 cup

Melt butter and white chocolate over simmering water in the top of a double boiler, in a saucepan on a heat diffuser, or in a microwave oven. When melted, remove from heat and whisk into a smooth, even mass. Whisk in extract. Measure cookie crumbs into food processor. Add nuts. Process together for 5-second intervals, checking texture frequently. It should be fine and dry, but not mushy. Add crumb/nut mixture all at once to butter mixture. Mash together with a fork until well blended and then deposit in springform. Press and flatten walnut-sized nuggets of crust mix no more than 1¹/2 inches up the sides of the springform pan, and spread remainder over bottom, pressing and smoothing it down with the back of a soup spoon. For a more detailed explanation of how to blend and lay down the crust, see page 158.

Filling

10″ SPRINGFORM		8″ SPRINGFORM
5 ounces	White chocolate	3 ounces
1 pound (two 8-ounce packages	Cream cheese	½ pound (one 8-ounce package)
1 can (about 1⅓ cups)	Sweetened condensed milk	½ can (about ⅔ cup)
4 teaspoons	Fruit Fresh	2 teaspoons
2 tablespoons	Fresh lemon juice	1 tablespoon
2 tablespoons	Framboise	1 tablespoon
	Reserved rhubarb	

Melt white chocolate over simmering water in the top of a double boiler, in a saucepan on a heat diffuser, or in a microwave oven, and reserve.

In a mixer, whip cream cheese on highest speed for 5 minutes. Add condensed milk and beat on medium speed for 2 minutes more, or until creamy and well blended. Dissolve Fruit Fresh in lemon juice. Add with chocolate and framboise to mixer bowl and beat until blended. *Or:*

In a food processor, whip up cream cheese and condensed milk using the on-off pulse about 25 times, and then just run the processor for 10 to 15 seconds more, or until ingredients are smooth and blended. Dissolve Fruit Fresh in lemon juice. Add with chocolate and framboise to processor bowl and blend well.

Fold in rhubarb. Pour into crust. Spread batter around carefully with a rubber spatula so that it's level and pressed firmly against the crust.

Garnish

½ cup fresh or frozen defrosted raspberries

Grated coconut

Decorate top of cake with raspberries and sprinkle with a handful of coconut. Put in refrigerator to set.

For an explanation of how to remove the cake from the springform, see page 159.

MOTHER WONDERFUL'S
NO-BAKE CRANCHERRY CHEESECAKE

Crust

10″ SPRINGFORM		8″ SPRINGFORM
2 1/2 *tablespoons*	Lightly salted butter	1 3/4 *tablespoons*
5 *ounces*	White chocolate	3 *ounces*
3/4 *cup*	Finely ground vanilla wafer crumbs	1/2 *cup*
3/4 *cup*	Almonds, chopped medium fine	1/2 *cup*

Melt butter and chocolate over simmering water in the top of a double boiler, in a saucepan on a heat diffuser, or in a microwave oven. When melted, remove from heat and whisk into a smooth, even mass. Measure cookie crumbs into food processor. Add nuts. Process together for 5-second intervals, checking texture frequently. It should be fine and dry, but not mushy. Add crumb/nut mixture all at once to butter mixture. Mash together with a fork until well blended and then deposit in springform. Press and flatten walnut-sized nuggets of crust mix no more than 1 1/2 inches up the sides of the springform pan, and spread remainder over bottom, pressing and smoothing it down with the back of a soup spoon. For a more detailed explanation of how to blend and lay down crust, see page 158.

Filling

10″ SPRINGFORM		8″ SPRINGFORM
5 ounces	White chocolate	3 ounces
1 pound (two 8-ounce packages)	Cream cheese	1/2 pound (one 8-ounce package)
1 can (about 1 1/3 cups)	Sweetened condensed milk	1/2 can (about 2/3 cup)
2 tablespoons	Fruit Fresh	1 tablespoon
3 tablespoons	Fresh lemon juice	1 1/2 tablespoons
2 tablespoons	Cranberry juice concentrate, or cranberry liqueur, or frozen cranberry juice concentrate undiluted	1 tablespoon
2 teaspoons	Cranberry extract	1 teaspoon
1 1/2 cups	Drained, tart, pitted canned cherries	3/4 cup

Melt chocolate over simmering water in the top of a double boiler, in a saucepan on a heat diffuser, or in a microwave oven, and reserve.

In a mixer, whip cream cheese on highest speed for 5 minutes. Add condensed milk and beat on medium speed for 2 minutes more, until creamy and well blended. Dissolve Fruit Fresh in lemon juice and add to mixer bowl along with cranberry concentrate or liqueur, extract, and melted chocolate. Beat briefly until blended. Or:

In a food processor, whip up cream cheese and condensed milk using the on-off pulse 25 times, and then just run the processor for 10 to 15 seconds more, or until ingredients are smooth and blended. Dissolve Fruit Fresh in lemon juice and concentrate or liqueur, then add to batter with extract and melted chocolate and process until well blended.

Fold in cherries with a rubber spatula. Pour into crust and spread batter around carefully and evenly so that it's level and pressed firmly against the crust.

Garnish

Grated coconut

Sprinkle with a handful of coconut and put into refrigerator to set.

For an explanation of how to remove the cake from the spring-form, see page 159.

MOTHER WONDERFUL'S
NO-BAKE HOLIDAY PUMPKIN CHEESECAKE

Crust

10″ SPRINGFORM		8″ SPRINGFORM
3 tablespoons	Lightly salted butter	2 tablespoons
3 ounces	White chocolate	2 ounces
1 teaspoon	Good brandy	3/4 teaspoon
3/4 cup	Finely ground ginger snap or spiced wafer crumbs	1/2 cup
3/4 cup	Walnuts, chopped medium fine	1/2 cup

Melt butter and white chocolate over simmering water in the top of a double boiler, in a saucepan on a heat diffuser, or in a microwave oven. When melted, remove from heat and whisk into a smooth, even mass. Whisk in brandy. Measure cookie crumbs into food processor. Add nuts. Process together for 5-second intervals, checking texture frequently. It should be fine and dry, but not mushy. Add crumb/nut mixture all at once to butter mixture. Mash together with a fork until well blended and then deposit in springform. Press and flatten walnut-sized nuggets of crust mix no more than 1½ inches up the sides of the springform pan, and spread remainder over bottom, pressing and smoothing it down with the back of a soup spoon. For a more detailed explanation of how to blend and lay down the crust, see page 158.

Filling

10″ SPRINGFORM		8″ SPRINGFORM
1 pound (two 8-ounce packages)	Cream cheese	½ pound (one 8-ounce package)
1 can (about 1⅓ cups)	Sweetened condensed milk	½ can (about ⅔ cup)
1 cup	Canned pumpkin	½ cup
2 teaspoons	Fruit Fresh	1 teaspoon
⅓ cup	Frozen orange juice concentrate, undiluted	2½ tablespoons
2 tablespoons	Fresh lemon juice	1 tablespoon
1 teaspoon	Good brandy	½ teaspoon
¾ teaspoon	Cinnamon	¼ teaspoon
⅛ teaspoon	Ground mace	pinch
pinch	Nutmeg	pinch
2 tablespoons	Maple syrup	1 tablespoon
¼ cup	Chopped walnuts	2 tablespoons
1 ounce	Crystallized ginger, thinly sliced or finely diced	½ ounce

In a mixer, whip cream cheese on highest speed for 5 minutes. Add condensed milk and pumpkin and beat on medium speed for 2 minutes more, or until creamy and well blended. Dissolve Fruit Fresh in juices and brandy and add with all remaining ingredients to mixer bowl. Beat briefly until well blended. *Or:*

In a food processor, whip up cream cheese and condensed milk using the on-off pulse about 25 times, and then just run the processor for 10 to 15 seconds more, or until ingredients are smooth and blended. Dissolve Fruit Fresh in juices and brandy and add with pumpkin, spices, and maple syrup to processor bowl and blend well. Fold in walnuts and ginger.

Pour into crust. Spread batter around carefully with a rubber spatula so that it's level and pressed firmly against the crust.

Garnish

Thinly sliced crystallized ginger

Place ginger slices around the top of the cheesecake like the numbers on a clock face and put into refrigerator to set.

If you want something especially festive

1/2 cup whipping cream

1 tablespoon confectioners' sugar

1 teaspoon good brandy

Finely chopped crystallized ginger

About 2 hours before cake is to be served, whip up cream, sugar, and brandy, spread over filling (or fit pastry bag with star tube and dab top of cake with whipped cream rosettes) and sprinkle with ginger. Keep cake refrigerated until just ready to serve.

For an explanation of how to remove the cake from the springform, see page 159.

Chic Cheesecake Muffins

READ BEFORE MAKING!

Muffins are chic this year, and where there is chic there should be cheesecake. Cheesecake muffins (or call them cupcakes, I don't care) should come in kooky, fun flavors. As you'll see in the following recipes, my imagination has run wild.

Cheesecake muffins are perfect for a child's party. They travel well, so you can pack them in a lunch box or take them picnicking. They also freeze nicely, defrost quickly, and are ready to serve in a jiffy. And if you don't know whether your guests prefer chocolate, Irish cream, or raspberry, it's easy enough to serve all three.

The results of my investigation of muffin pans and cups indicate that there are variations in size and volume among several of those considered standard. These differences are itemized on the following chart:

MUFFIN SIZE	NUMBER PER PAN	DEPTH	DIAMETER
Giant	6	$1\frac{1}{4}''$	$3\frac{1}{4}''$
Standard #1	12	$1\frac{1}{4}''$	$2\frac{3}{4}''$
Standard #2	12	$1\frac{1}{8}''$	$1\frac{5}{8}''$
Aluminum throw-away Standard #3	6	$1\frac{1}{4}''$	$2\frac{3}{4}''$
Teensy	12	$\frac{7}{8}''$	$1\frac{3}{4}''$

Three tablespoons of crust mix will line any standard muffin cup, and ¼ cup of batter should satisfactorily fill one. For tiny muffinettes, one tablespoon of crust mix and a heaping tablespoon of filling should suffice. I only make muffinettes with no-bake fillings.

The following recipe proportions are for twelve muffins. If you want to make fewer, divide by two and just make six, or six of one kind and six of another.

No-Bake Cheescake Muffins

Naturally, I prefer no-bake cheesecake muffins because they're easier to make and there's no waiting period while they bake and cool. Consequently, nine of the following ten cheesecake muffins are also no-bake. They contain a small amount of batter, so they set quickly. They should set in the refrigerator, but if you're in a real hurry, put them directly into the freezer for 30–40 minutes and they'll be edible. I try to freeze three from each batch of a dozen I make so I can serve assorted flavors later. Do this, and your friends will also marvel at your culinary legerdemain.

No-bake batter can be beaten in a mixer, but since each batch of filling (twelve muffins worth) contains only 8–11 ounces of cream cheese, a food processor will provide a smoother, more uniform batter.

You may well ask, what should one do if one has no food processor? The answer is simple:

GET ONE!
GET ONE!
GET ONE!

Lining each muffin tin cup with a paper baking cup enhances a muffin's appearance. Naturally, I tried the fancy, expensive, imported cup liners first, but in the end I prefer the Sweetheart foil-laminated baking cups (2½-inch diameter) that were for sale at my déclassé neighborhood supermarket. Some cup liners will be slightly wider than the muffin cups and may jut out of the tins initially, but the lining of crust will stabilize and solidify them. I prefer to make my no-bake muffins in the aluminum throwaway tins because the baking cup liners fit those muffin cups best. I freeze my leftover no-bake muffins in the throwaway tins as well, because the tins stack so nicely in the freezer and can be used over and over without serious washing.

For no-bake muffins, metal cups can also be lined with a 6-inch square of plastic wrap. Tiny muffinette cups should be lined only with plastic wrap. The overhang helps you lift out the set, chilled cheesecake muffin. Naturally you'll strip off the plastic wrap before serving. If you press crust mix against a naked metal muffin cup, you may have to run a sharp knife around the sides to remove the finished muffin, but there's enough butter in the crust to keep it from sticking once the crust stands at room temperature for a few minutes.

If you're afraid your fingers are too klutzy to maneuver those crumbs around the baking cup or muffin tin, relax and remember the basic rule of crumb crusts: Press small amounts of the mix against the sides of the muffin cup first. Another helpful technique is to flatten a nugget of crust mix against the side of your mixing bowl and then transfer this flattened slab to the sides of your muffin cup. Wrapping your fingers in plastic wrap will help control a buttery crust.

Since my crust mix proportions are generous, you may have leftovers. Never discard these leftovers. Instead, line additional cup liners with crust mix, chill them, stack them, wrap them in foil, and freeze them. If you have only a small amount, make crusts for muffinettes. At some future date, when you have surplus batter, you can fill those perfectly good pre-frozen crusts with it.

Leftover crust mix can also be frozen *au naturel* in a glob. Later, different batches can be zapped and warmed in the microwave, individually or together. Leftover crust mix can extend a skimpy crust. Suppose you have all the batter ingredients but are missing something for a crust; zap all those leftover crust globs and, voilà, there's your crust.

Notice that I specify finely ground nuts for the no-bake cheesecake muffin crust mix. The finer and mushier the crust blend, the more easily it sculpts into a cup.

Baked Muffins

Baked cheesecake muffins can be prepared in a foil or paper baking cup too. Muffin cups can also be lined with a 6-inch square sheet of aluminum foil. A third alternative is to lay a $1'' \times 7''$ strip of aluminum foil down the side across the bottom and up the other side of a muffin cup like a stirrup. Press your crust into the cup, fill it with batter, bake, and chill. When the muffin is ready to serve, let it sit at room temperature for a few minutes and then pull on both ends of the stirrup to lift the muffin out.

Cheesecake Muffins

GINGER PEACHY NO-BAKE
CHEESECAKE MUFFINS

Crust

5 tablespoons lightly
  salted butter

6 ounces white chocolate

1 cup finely ground
  gingersnap crumbs

1 cup finely ground pine
  nuts

Melt butter and chocolate together over simmering water in the top
of a double boiler, in a saucepan on a heat diffuser, or in a microwave
oven, and reserve. Blend crumbs and nuts together in a food processor and then add chocolate mixture and pulse until well combined.
Line the cups of a muffin tin with plastic wrap or foil-laminated
baking cups and press crust mix all around to sheathe the cups. Use
your fingers (protecting them with plastic wrap if necessary) or use
the back of a spoon to smooth and even out the crust. Three tablespoons will do the trick. Start with 2 tablespoons of crust mix and
completely cover the sides of each baking cup with it, and then use

the remaining tablespoon of the crust mix to fill in the bottom of each cup. Refrigerate pan to firm up crusts. Label and freeze any leftover crust mix.

Filling

One 8-ounce package cream cheese	1 large fresh peach or nectarine
⅔ cup sweetened condensed milk	⅓ cup ginger marmalade
⅓ cup fresh lime juice	Fruit Fresh

Blend cream cheese, condensed milk, and lime juice together well in a food processor. Cut fruit into slices and reserve a fourth of the fruit for the tops of the filled muffins. Add marmalade and fruit to batter and pulse on-off 5 times, to chop slightly and fold in. Pour batter into crust cups. Sprinkle reserved peach slices with Fruit Fresh and insert one slice into the top of each muffin to decorate and identify them, in case you freeze some and later don't remember what flavor they are.

GRAPEFRUIT NO-BAKE CHEESECAKE MUFFINS

I happen to really like this flavor. I think it is subtle and elegant.

Crust

5 tablespoons lightly salted butter	1 cup finely chopped vanilla wafer crumbs
6 ounces white chocolate	
1 cup finely chopped walnuts	

Melt butter and chocolate together over simmering water in the top of a double boiler, in a saucepan on a heat diffuser, or in a microwave oven, and reserve. Blend crumbs and nuts together in a food processor and then add chocolate mixture and pulse until well combined. Line each cup of a muffin tin with plastic wrap or insert a foil-laminated baking cup, and press crust mix all around to sheathe it. Smooth and even out the crust. Three tablespoons of crust per muffin will do the trick. Refrigerate pan. Label and freeze any leftover crust mix.

Filling

3 ounces white chocolate	¼ cup frozen grapefruit juice concentrate, undiluted
11 ounces (one 8-ounce package + one 3-ounce package) cream cheese	
	1½ tablespoons grapefruit extract
1 cup sweetened condensed milk	2 tablespoons Fruit Fresh

Melt chocolate over simmering water in the top of a double boiler, in a saucepan on a heat diffuser, or in a microwave oven, and reserve. Process cream cheese and sweetened condensed milk in food processor until smooth and creamy. Dissolve Fruit Fresh in grapefruit juice. Add to processor along with melted chocolate extract and blend well. Fill each crust cup with about ¼ cup of batter.

Garnish

Grapefruit-flavored jellied candies
Fresh or canned drained grapefruit segments
Fruit Fresh

Decorate each muffin with a grapefruit-flavored jellied candy or a segment of fresh grapefruit. If you choose fresh grapefruit, sprinkle segments with Fruit Fresh to keep them from turning brown. Refrigerate to set.

CHOCOLATE RASPBERRY
NO-BAKE CHEESECAKE MUFFINS

Crust

4 tablespoons (½ stick) lightly salted butter

1 pound chocolate-covered pretzels: a mixture of equal amounts of milk chocolate-, dark chocolate-, and white chocolate-covered pretzels

2 cups finely chopped walnuts

Melt butter and reserve, but use it while it is warm. Blend chocolate-covered pretzels and nuts together in a food processor and then add melted butter and pulse until well combined. Line each cup of a muffin tin with plastic wrap or insert a foil-laminated baking cup and press crust mix all around to sheathe it. Smooth and even out the crust. Three tablespoons of crust per muffin will do the trick. Refrigerate pan. Label and freeze any leftover crust mix.

Filling

2 ounces dark chocolate

1 pound (two 8-ounce packages) cream cheese

1 cup sweetened condensed milk

⅔ cup frozen raspberry daiquiri concentrate, undiluted

Melt chocolate over simmering water in the top of a double boiler, in a saucepan on a heat diffuser, or in a microwave oven, and reserve. Process cream cheese, sweetened condensed milk, melted chocolate, and raspberry daiquiri concentrate in a food processor until smooth and creamy. Fill each crust cup with about ¼ cup of batter.

Garnish

Fresh raspberries sprinkled with Fruit Fresh

Decorate with a few fresh raspberries that have been sprinkled with Fruit Fresh to prevent them from turning brown. Refrigerate to set.

IRISH CREAM NO-BAKE CHEESECAKE MUFFINS

Crust

4 ounces dark chocolate

1 ounce white chocolate

3 tablespoons lightly salted butter

1 cup shortbread cookie crumbs

1 cup finely chopped Brazil nuts

Melt butter and both kinds of chocolate together over simmering water in the top of a double boiler, in a saucepan on a heat diffuser, or in a microwave oven, and reserve. Blend cookie crumbs and nuts together in a food processor and then add butter/chocolate mix and pulse until well combined. Line each cup of a muffin tin with plastic wrap or insert a foil-laminated baking cup and press crust mix all around to sheathe it. Smooth and even out the crust. Three tablespoons of crust per muffin will do the trick. Refrigerate pan. Label and freeze any leftover crust mix.

Filling

3 ounces white chocolate

11 ounces (one 8-ounce package + one 3-ounce package) cream cheese

2/3 cup sweetened condensed milk

2 tablespoons Irish cream liqueur

1 tablespoon Irish cream extract

Melt chocolate over simmering water in the top of a double boiler, in a saucepan on a heat diffuser, or in a microwave oven, and reserve. Process cream cheese, sweetened condensed milk, melted chocolate, Irish cream liqueur, and extract in a food processor until smooth and creamy. Fill each crust cup with about ¼ cup of batter.

Garnish

Shaved dark chocolate

Decorate with shaved chocolate and refrigerate to set.

PRETZELS, ROOT BEER, AND JELLY BEAN NO-BAKE CHEESECAKE MUFFINS

Crust

6 tablespoons (¾ stick) lightly salted butter

6 ounces white chocolate

2 ounces dark, sweet, or semisweet chocolate

12 ounces pretzels, unsalted or with salt brushed off

1½ cups finely chopped Brazil nuts

Melt butter and both kinds of chocolate together over simmering water in the top of a double boiler, in a saucepan on a heat diffuser, or in a microwave oven, and reserve. Process pretzels, blend well with nuts in a food processor, and then add chocolate mixture and pulse until well combined. Line each cup of a muffin tin with plastic wrap or insert a foil-laminated baking cup and press crust mix all around to sheathe it. Smooth and even out the crust. Three table-spoons of crust per muffin will do the trick. Refrigerate pan. Label and freeze any leftover crust mix.

Filling

3 ounces white chocolate

11 ounces (one 8-ounce package + one 3-ounce package) cream cheese

⅔ cup sweetened condensed milk

2 teaspoons Fruit Fresh

2 tablespoons white grape juice concentrate, undiluted

2 tablespoons root beer flavoring

3 drops yellow food coloring

Melt chocolate over simmering water in the top of a double boiler, in a saucepan on a heat diffuser, or in a microwave oven, and reserve. Process cream cheese and sweetened condensed milk in a food processor until smooth and creamy. Dissolve Fruit Fresh in grape juice. Add to processor with root beer flavoring, melted chocolate, and food coloring and process till well combined. Fill each crust cup with about ¼ cup of batter.

Garnish

Jelly Beans

Scatter jelly beans on top and refrigerate to set.

PRUNE DANISH
NO-BAKE CHEESECAKE MUFFINS

Crust

¼ pound (1 stick) lightly salted butter

4 ounces white chocolate

1½ cups finely ground Danish butter cookie crumbs

1½ cups finely chopped blanched almonds

Melt butter and chocolate together over simmering water in the top of a double boiler, in a saucepan on a heat diffuser, or in a microwave oven, and reserve. Blend cookie crumbs and nuts in a food processor and then add chocolate mixture and pulse until well combined. Line each cup of a muffin tin with plastic wrap or insert a foil-laminated baking cup and press crust mix all around to sheathe it. Smooth and even out the crust. Three tablespoons of crust per muffin will do the trick. Refrigerate pan. Label and freeze any leftover crust mix.

Filling

1 pound (two 8-ounce packages) cream cheese	1/3 cup fresh lemon juice
1 can (about 1 1/3 cups) sweetened condensed milk	1/4 cup prune cake filling or lekvar

Blend cream cheese, sweetened condensed milk, and lemon juice in a food processor until smooth and creamy. Spread 1 teaspoon of prune filling in the bottom of each muffin cup, then fill the cups with batter, about 1/4 cup to each.

Garnish

1/4 cup prune cake filling or lekvar

Dab 1 teaspoon of prune filling in the center of each muffin so it looks like the topping of a Danish pastry. Refrigerate to set.

AMARETTO ALMOND
NO-BAKE CHEESECAKE MUFFINS

I made these in individual readymade crusts, which is acceptable only in the direst emergencies. This amount of batter will fill 6 individual readymade crusts. If you use your own crusts, this amount of batter will fill 12.

Crust

¼ pound (1 stick) lightly salted butter	1½ cups finely chopped blanched almonds
4 ounces white chocolate	
1½ cups finely ground shortbread cookie crumbs	

Melt butter and chocolate together over simmering water in the top of a double boiler, in a saucepan on a heat diffuser, or in a microwave oven, and reserve. Blend cookie crumbs and nuts in a food processor and then add chocolate mixture and pulse until well combined. Line each cup of a muffin tin with plastic wrap or insert a foil-laminated baking cup and press crust mix all around to sheathe it. Smooth and even out the crust. Three tablespoons of crust per muffin will do the trick. Refrigerate pan. Label and freeze any leftover crust mix.

Filling

4 ounces white chocolate	3 tablespoons amaretto liqueur
½ pound (one 8-ounce package) cream cheese	¼ teaspoon amaretto extract
⅔ cup sweetened condensed milk	¾ cup sliced almonds, with skin
2 teaspoons Fruit Fresh	
1 tablespoon orange juice concentrate, undiluted	

Melt chocolate over simmering water in the top of a double boiler, in a saucepan on a heat diffuser, or in a microwave oven, and reserve. process cream cheese and sweetened condensed milk in a food processor until smooth and creamy. Dissolve Fruit Fresh in orange juice. Add to processor with amaretto, amaretto extract, and melted chocolate and process till well combined. Fold in nuts. Fill each crust cup with about ¼ cup of batter.

Garnish

Sliced almonds, with skin

Sprinkle almonds on top and refrigerate to set.

HALLOWEEN
NO-BAKE CHEESECAKE MUFFINS

Crust

9 tablespoons lightly
  salted butter (1 stick +
  1 tablespoon)

8 ounces white chocolate

2 ounces dark chocolate

3 cups finely chopped
  caramel corn

1 cup chopped peanuts

Melt butter and both chocolates together over simmering water in the top of a double boiler, in a saucepan on a heat diffuser, or in a microwave oven, and reserve. Chop up caramel corn and peanuts as finely as you can in a food processor. Don't be alarmed if you can't. This crust tends to be bulky. Add chocolate mixture and pulse until well combined. Line each cup of a muffin tin with plastic wrap or insert a foil-laminated baking cup and press crust mix all around to sheathe it. Smooth and even out the crust. Refrigerate pan. Label and freeze any leftover crust mix. (I made this in foil-laminated cups and they required a lot of crust. Don't be stingy.) The recipe produces lots of crust mix, so make the sides very firm. It might be helpful if you wrap your hand in plastic wrap and press each nugget of mix against the side of the processor bowl to flatten it before pressing it against the side of the foil cup.

Filling

½ pound (one 8-ounce package) cream cheese

⅔ cup sweetened condensed milk

1 tablespoon Fruit Fresh

⅓ cup frozen orange juice concentrate, undiluted

5 dots red food coloring

10 dots yellow food coloring

Process cream cheese and sweetened condensed milk in a food processor until smooth and creamy. Dissolve Fruit Fresh in orange juice. Add to processor with food coloring and process till well combined. Fill crust cups with filling. Because these crusts are thick, they will need little more than ⅛ cup of filling.

Garnish

12 pumpkin faces or other Halloween candies

Press 1 candy into middle of each muffin and refrigerate to set.

CHOCOLATE NUT
NO-BAKE CHEESECAKE MUFFINS

Crust

4½ tablespoons lightly salted butter

9 ounces chocolate nonpareils

¾ cup chopped shortbread crumbs

1½ cups chopped hazelnuts

Melt butter and chocolate nonpareils together over simmering water in the top of a double boiler, in a saucepan on a heat diffuser, or in a microwave oven, and reserve. Blend cookie crumbs and nuts in a food processor and then add chocolate mixture and pulse until well combined. Line each cup of a muffin tin with plastic wrap or insert a foil-laminated baking cup and press crust mix all around to sheathe it. Smooth and even out the crust. Three tablespoons of crust per muffin will do the trick. Refrigerate pan. Label and freeze any leftover crust mix.

Filling

3 ounces white chocolate

11 ounces cream cheese (one 8-ounce package + one 3-ounce package)

1 scant cup sweetened condensed milk

2 tablespoons crème de cacao

2 tablespoons praline liqueur

4 teaspoons Fruit Fresh

1½ tablespoons orange juice concentrate, undiluted

¾ cup coarsely chopped hazelnuts

2 ounces shaved semisweet chocolate

Melt white chocolate over simmering water in the top of a double boiler, in a saucepan on a heat diffuser, or in a microwave oven, and reserve. Process cream cheese, sweetened condensed milk, crème de cacao and praline liqueur in a food processor until smooth and creamy. Dissolve Fruit Fresh in orange juice. Add to processor and blend well. Fold in hazelnuts and shaved chocolate. Fill each crust cup with about ¼ cup of batter.

Garnish

¼ cup Nutella* or

Shaved chocolate

*See page 90.

Swirl 1 teaspoon of Nutella (chocolate-hazelnut spread) into the top of each muffin. If you can't find Nutella, sprinkle with more shaved chocolate.

BASIC BAKED
CHEESECAKE MUFFINS

Preheat oven to 350° F.
Ingredients need not be at room temperature.

Line each muffin tin with a foil-laminated baking cup or cut a 1″ × 7″ strip of aluminum foil and run it across the bottom and sides like a stirrup.

Crust

¼ pound (1 stick) lightly
  salted butter
2 cups vanilla wafer
  crumbs

¼ cup sugar

Melt butter over very low heat. Combine butter with crumbs and sugar in a food processor until thoroughly blended, or stir and mash together with a fork in a roomy bowl. Press small amounts of crust mix all the way up the sides of ungreased muffin cups and then over the bottom.

Filling

1 pound (two 8-ounce
  packages) cream cheese
¾ cup sugar

2¼ teaspoons fresh lime
  or lemon juice
2 large eggs

In a mixer, whip cream cheese on the highest speed for 5 minutes, then add sugar and whip for 2 minutes more. Add citrus juice and blend in thoroughly. Add the eggs, one at a time, keeping the mixer on the *lowest speed* in order to prevent too much air from destroying the proper consistency of the batter; mix just until each egg has been incorporated into the batter. *Or:*

If using a food processor, put the sugar in first. Cut each 8-ounce block of cream cheese into eight 1-inch cubes and add the first 8 cubes to bowl. Process using on-off pulse about 25 times, and then add the rest of the cream cheese cubes gradually, blending them in with on-off pulses until mixture is smooth and creamy. When you think it's perfect, blend nonstop for 20 seconds more, then blend in citrus juice for 5 seconds. Crack eggs in a bowl, break them up slightly with a fork, add them to batter in processor bowl, and fold them lightly into batter with a rubber spatula to prevent them from sinking to the bottom. Cut the eggs into the batter by using the on-off pulse 5 times, then scrape down the sides with a rubber spatula and pulse on-off 5 times more.

Pour batter into muffin crusts and bake in preheated oven for 8 minutes. Remove from oven and let stand on a counter for 2 minutes before putting on the glaze.

Sour Cream Glaze

½ cup sour cream

1 tablespoon sugar

¼ teaspoon almond extract

Combine sour cream, sugar, and extract with a rubber spatula in a plastic bowl. Spread evenly and smoothly over tops of muffins and return to 350° F oven for 2 minutes. Remove from oven and *immediately* place in refrigerator to cool.

If you haven't lined each cup with a baking cup, let cupcakes stand at room temperature for a few minutes to allow the butter to loosen its bond with the metal. Separate the sides from the metal with a warm sharp knife and pull up on the foil stirrups. The crust will usually detach easily from the sides.

Magic Formula Bonus

Incidentally, you can make muffins out of any of the baked cheese-cake recipes. For each dozen, here's the magic formula:

Crust

The amount of crust mix required for the larger (10″) cake.

Filling

The amount of filling required for the smaller (8″) cake.

Baking Time

Bake for 8 minutes at 350° F. Let sit on counter top for 2 minutes before spreading on glaze. If you don't want to bother with a glaze, refrigerate muffins after a 2-minute rest.

Sour Cream Glaze

½ cup sour cream   ¼ teaspoon extract
1 tablespoon sugar

That should provide you with a tablespoon or so of glaze for each of the dozen muffins. Bake for 2 minutes more and refrigerate.

Tricks for Lower-Calorie Cheesecakes

Let's not kid ourselves. If God had wanted cheesecake to be a diet aid, he would have made butterfat noncaloric. I hope you've noticed that I hid that unpleasant fact in the middle of the book, where you really have to dig to find it. However, cheesecakes can be less caloric if you have a few tools and a few tricks up your sleeve, and can think fearlessly. They will not taste as rich and as sweet as the ones you've read about on previous pages, but they will be quite edible and far less guilt-producing.

Necessary Tools and Implements

The tools include a surgical mask (not for purity, but to keep your mouth off-limits). Working in rubber gloves is also helpful. I've never seen any cook lick batter off those. A sink full of soapy water is another must, so you can defile your mixing pans before that leftover batter defiles your lips. Remember, only skinny blondes with thick, straight hair are born loving low-calorie wonders like apricots, coffee, and raspberries. The rest of us must acquire a taste for them—and never really prefer them to fudge. The other essential implement is a food processor, to whip the blazes out of whatever inferior substitute you're using to replace the more caloric and tastier cream cheese, so that even if you have far less butterfat than in a regular cheese-cake, at least you'll have the same texture and appearance.

Trick Number One

Despite what you may secretly believe, all cookie crumbs are high in calories. I thought there were big differences, and that zwieback had lots fewer calories than vanilla wafers because it tastes dry and gritty. No way. The cookie crumb maven at Nabisco told me it ain't so. Cookies crumble at the rate of 400 to 600 calories per cup. Here's proof positive from the horse's mouth:

Caloric Equivalents from One Cup of Fine Cookie Crumbs:

Chocolate Sandwich Cookies = 611 *calories*

Gingersnaps = 540 *calories*

Chocolate chip cookies = 517 *calories*

Shortbread cookies = 490 *calories*

Vanilla wafers = 475 *calories*

Chocolate wafers = 468 *calories*

Graham crackers = 420 *calories*

Zwieback = 400 *calories*

Read it and weep.

I suppose you could make a crust out of colored, flavored saw-dust, but there is a tastier solution. Make your crust out of cereal crumbs. They're sweet but lower in calories, and if they're loaded with additives and preservatives, so are the higher-calorie cookie crumbs.

To give you an idea of the difference, for an 8-inch cheesecake made with 1 pound of whatever cheese (the size I prefer for these lower-calorie cheesecakes), you need about 1¼ cups of crumbs. The cereal crumbs tally about 110 calories per ounce, which grind down to 220 calories a cup. You don't have to be a math major to see the saving in calories. You can forgo any additional sugar (just add two packs of artificial sweetener if you feel the need), but you can't forgo one crumb. You have to really press the crust mixture into the sides and dig out any excess from the angle where the sides meet the bottom. The best way to make these crusts go farther is to smooth them and even them by fitting in a sheet of plastic wrap and pressing the crusts under it with the back of a spoon. And here's a surprise for you: Caramel corn and Cracker Jacks are only 110 calories per ounce. Caramel corn grinds up into a 110-calorie cup of crumbs. I got so excited, I tried it in a crust, but nothing is perfect. It was very gummy and I didn't like working with it. I prefer sweet, crunchy, hard cereals like Honey Nut Cheerios and Cocoa Puffs.

Trick Number Two

Instead of using butter or margarine (100 calories per tablespoon) to bind the crumbs together, research showed that a dieter can make do with only 3 or 4 tablespoons of a light butter or margarine (50 to 60 calories per tablespoon) or Le Slim Cow (only 56 calories per tablespoon), which contains buttermilk. I prefer Land O Lakes Country Morning Blend Light because the taste and texture are more traditional, but I've used all, and any will do. Just make sure you give yourself the whole 200-calorie amount.

However, if you want to cut even more calories, make the cheesecake in a pie pan sprayed with vegetable oil spray instead of in a springform, and use only ⅓ cup cereal crumbs. Swirl the crumbs around so that a thin layer sticks to the sides of the pan, and spread the rest evenly over the bottom. The cheesecake batter will combine with the cereal and supply a somewhat undefined crust. Or eliminate the crumbs altogether and make the cheesecake in a vegetable oil–sprayed pan.

Trick Number Three

Make sure the fat really blends into the cereal crumbs in the processor and doesn't stick to the bottom of the bowl, so your crusts get every bit of butterfat they are entitled to. And remember, the warmer the crumbs are, the more manageable they are.

Trick Number Four

Stay away from whole eggs. I usually substitute 3 egg whites (17 calories each) for every 2 whole eggs (81 calories each) in a recipe. In addition to slightly reduced calories, you get monumentally reduced cholesterol. I see no reason to use cholesterol-free real egg products in cheesecake. They're just frozen, colored egg whites. You have to defrost them, and they cost a whole lot more.

Trick Number Five

Initially, I add half the amount of sugar I think a batter really requires to sweeten it properly, and then I make up the difference with artificial sweeteners. There's a new one on the market called Sunette Sweet One Low Calorie Sugar Substitute, which is sodium free and heat stable and hadn't created any diseases in its users when I turned in this manuscript, although since then it's been shown to increase blood-cholesterol levels in diabetic test animals, so avoid feeding it to your diabetic pets.

I like the taste of sugar, but if you don't, here are a few other substitutes you might employ. Fructose comes from the natural sugar found in fresh fruits and honey. It's approximately 50 percent sweeter than common sugar and is converted differently in the body. Unlike sugar, which passes through the liver and immediately enters the bloodstream, causing a rise in blood sugar level, fructose is trapped in the liver and stored as carbohydrate. It enters the bloodstream in an orderly time-delayed sequence. Because it causes less of an increase in blood sugar, it's acceptable for diabetics—up to 75 grams can be consumed by them a day, as long as it's accounted for on an exchange basis, that is, 1 teaspoon of fructose is equal to the carbohydrate portion of ½ fruit exchange. One cup of sugar has 960 calories. A comparably sweet amount of fructose (¾ cup) is a mere 550 calories.

Another possible substitute is Sucanat, which has 12 calories per teaspoon, as opposed to 20 in sugar, and tallies up to 576 calories per cup. It's simply evaporated cane juice.

If you wish to cut your sugar intake, you should taste these substitutes and make your own decision.

For artificial sweeteners, I use Sunette Sweet One in my baked low-calorie cheesecakes, but I prefer Equal in the unbaked cheesecakes. I like the flavor better, but Equal loses its sweetness when it's heated for a long period of time, so it's not ideal for baking.

Trick Number Six

Pure cream cheese is a no-no-no. Here's a list of possible substitutes.

CHEESE	CALORIES PER OUNCE	CALORIES PER POUND
Cream cheese	100	1600
Light cream cheese or neufchâtel	80	1280
Imitation cream cheese	60	960
Part-skim ricotta	45	720
Farmer cheese	40	640
Cottage cheese	30	480
Lowfat cottage cheese	23	368
Lowfat yogurt, drained overnight in a cone (8 ounce = 6½ ounces yogurt cheese)	23	368
Light 'n Lively or other light 1% cottage cheese	20	320

The trick with all of these is to really whip the blazes out of them in a food processor so that they have the texture of cream cheese. Then sweeten them enough to conceal the blandness that results from the reduction of fat. You can use one kind of cheese for each cake, or blend them together. Mix them and match them. It doesn't really matter as long as the proportions stay the same. They should bake in the same amount of time. You can even make no-bakes with them!

Trick Number Seven

Make these cakes in an 8-inch springform so your crumbs will go farther. Top them with sliced fresh fruit to make them look grand and elegant.

Trick Number Eight

Add fresh ripe fruits to the batter to extend the flavor without upping the caloric value very much.

Trick Number Nine

Except for fresh fruit, toppings are out! They're just too expensive, caloriewise, and really not necessary. Make the cake look fattening and beautiful by sprinkling on cocoa or a smidgen of grated chocolate right before serving, or something equally mouth-watering yet deceptive. And as a last resort there's always the tried-and-true disguise— powdering the top with confectioners' sugar so people will think they're eating something wunderbar.

Turn the page and see how these tricks actually work in practice. You'll have to follow instructions on these and blot and drain when I say so, because otherwise the cakes will be too watery and they won't cook fast enough.

Trick Number Ten

Make as small a cake as possible. Always make less than you think you'll need. You never want leftover cheesecake, even the low-cal kind, singing a siren song to you from the refrigerator 'round about midnight.

11

Lower-Calorie
Cheesecakes

LOWER-CALORIE PINEAPPLE
CHEESECAKE

Preheat oven to 350° F.
Coat 10-inch springform pan with vegetable oil spray.

Crust

¼ cup (4 tablespoons)
reduced-fat margarine
1¼ cups crumbs from
crispy brown rice cereal

1 tablespoon sugar
2 packets heat-stable
artificial sweetener

Melt margarine over very low heat and add it to the crumbs, sugar, and sweetener in a food processor and blend till well combined. Put all the crust mix in your springform pan and wrap plastic wrap over your fingers to help press the mix around the sides to a height of no more than 1 inch. Press remaining crust mix over the bottom of your pan. It may not stick perfectly, but do the best you can. I generally press it to a height of one inch against the sides and then use the back of a spoon to spread it onto the bottom, stealing from the sides until I have enough to cover the bottom. Set aside.

Filling and Garnish

8 ounces light cream cheese or neufchâtel

8 ounces part-skim-milk ricotta

1 teaspoon pineapple extract

1/4 cup sugar

8 packets heat-stable artificial sweetener

2 large egg whites

1/2 ounce sugarless dried or fresh pineapple, very thinly sliced

Blot excess water from cheeses with a paper towel. Whip up cheeses, extract, sugar, and sweetener in food processor until very creamy. Add egg whites and whip in with 5 to 7 on-off pulses. Fold in pineapple and pour into crust. Bake for 25 minutes. Cool in refrigerator. Decorate with thinly sliced dried sugarless pineapple or fresh pineapple slices.

CORY'S OLD-FASHIONED LIGHT CHEESECAKE

Preheat oven to 350° F.
Coat 8-inch springform pan with vegetable oil spray.

Crust

1/4 cup (4 tablespoons) reduced-fat margarine

1 1/2 cups fine Honeycomb (or similar) cereal crumbs

2 tablespoons sugar

3 packets heat-stable artificial sweetener

1 teaspoon cinnamon

1 tablespoon chopped toasted almonds

Melt margarine over very low heat and then add it to the crumbs, sugar, sweetener, and cinnamon in a food processor and blend until well combined. Mix ¼ cup crumbs with nuts and reserve to sprinkle on top of baked cake. Put all the rest of the crust mix into the springform and wrap plastic wrap over your fingers to help press the mix around the sides to the height of 1½ inches. Then press remaining crust mix over the bottom of your pan. Set aside.

Filling and Garnish

¾ pound farmer cheese

4 ounces neufchâtel or light cream cheese

¼ cup sugar

6 packets heat-stable artificial sweetener

1 teaspoon vanilla

1 teaspoon rum extract

½ teaspoon black walnut extract

4 large egg whites

Confectioners' sugar for garnish

Blot excess liquid from cheeses with paper towel. Whip up cheeses, sugar, sweetener, and extracts in a food processor until very smooth and creamy. When you think it looks and acts like cream cheese, process it for 10 seconds more. Add egg whites and blend until just incorporated—15 on-off pulses. Pour into crust and bake for 20 minutes. Sprinkle reserved crust on top and refrigerate at once to cool. Sprinkle with confectioners' sugar before serving.

LOWER-CALORIE
BUTTERCARAMEL NUT CHEESECAKE

Preheat oven to 350° F.
Coat 8-inch springform pan with vegetable oil spray.

Crust

3 tablespoons reduced-fat
  margarine
1½ cups Crunchy Nut
  Oh's (or similar) cereal
  crumbs

1 tablespoon sugar
2 packets heat-stable
  artificial sweetener

Melt margarine over very low heat and then add it to the crumbs, sugar, and sweetener in a food processor and blend till well combined. Put all the crumbs into the springform and wrap plastic wrap over your fingers to help press the mix around the sides to the height of no more than 1 inch. Then press remaining crust mix over the bottom of your pan. Set aside.

Filling and Garnish

8 ounces part-skim-milk
  ricotta
8 ounces neufchâtel
¼ cup sugar
6 packets heat-stable
  artificial sweetener
¾ teaspoon caramel
  extract

½ teaspoon butterscotch
  extract
2 large egg whites
1 tablespoon slivered
  almonds
1 tablespoon caramel ice-
  cream topping

Blend cheeses, sugar, sweetener, and extracts in food processor until very creamy. Add egg whites and whip in quickly with 5 to 7 on-off pulses. Pour into crust. Bake for 22 minutes. Sprinkle almonds on top, dribble caramel topping around them, and refrigerate.

LOWER-CALORIE APRICOT CHEESECAKE

Preheat oven to 350° F.
Coat 8-inch springform pan with vegetable oil spray.

Crust

¼ cup (4 tablespoons)
reduced-fat margarine

1½ cup crumbs from a
sweet, crunchy cereal

1 tablespoon sugar

2 packages heat-stable
artificial sweetener

Melt margarine over very low heat and then add it to the crumbs, sugar, and sweetener in a food processor and blend till well combined. Reserve 1 tablespoon crust mix for topping. Put all the crumbs in the springform pan and wrap plastic wrap over your fingers to help press the mix around the sides to the height of no more than 1 inch. Then press remaining mix over the bottom of the pan. Set aside.

Filling and Garnish

One 8-ounce can low-
calorie apricot halves

1 pound farmer cheese

⅓ cup sugar

3 packets heat-stable
artificial sweetener

1½ teaspoons brandy
extract

3 large egg whites

¼ cup low-calorie apricot
preserves

Drain and blot apricot halves. Discard syrup, reserve three halves for topping, and cut the remainder into chunks. Process cheese, sugar, sweetener, and 1¼ teaspoons extract until very smooth. Add egg whites and apricot chunks and whip into batter in 7 on-off pulses. Pour into crust. Slice reserved apricots in long thin slices and decorate top of cake. Sprinkle with reserved crust mix crumbs. Bake for 20 minutes. Put into refrigerator to cool. When cool, process ¼ cup low-calorie apricot preserves with ¼ teaspoon brandy extract and glaze top with a brush.

LOWER-CALORIE VERMONT APPLE CHEESECAKE

Preheat oven to 350° F.
Coat 8-inch springform pan with vegetable oil spray.

Crust

3½ tablespoons reduced-
   fat margarine
1½ cups crumbs from
   Apple Jacks cereal

1 tablespoon sugar
2 packets heat-stable
   artificial sweetener
1 teaspoon cinnamon

Melt margarine over very low heat and then add it to the crumbs, sugar, sweetener, and cinnamon in a food processor and blend till well combined. Put all the crumbs into the springform and wrap plastic wrap over your fingers to help press the mix around the sides to the height of no more than 1 inch. Then press remaining mix over the bottom of the pan. Set aside.

Filling

8 ounces neufchâtel
4 ounces farmer cheese
4 ounces part-skim-milk
   ricotta
¼ cup sugar
3 packets heat-stable
   artificial sweetener

¾ teaspoon maple
   flavoring
2 large egg whites
1 pack Weight Watchers
   dried apple snacks
½ teaspoon cinnamon

Blend cheeses, sugar, sweetener, and maple flavoring in food processor until very creamy. Whip in egg whites with 7 to 10 on-off pulses.

Dredge apple snacks in cinnamon and fold into batter. Pour into crust. Bake for 20 minutes. Cool in refrigerator.

LOWER-CALORIE MOCHA MIST CHEESECAKE

Preheat oven to 350° F.
Coat 10-inch springform pan with vegetable oil spray.

Crust

3½ tablespoons reduced-fat margarine

1½ cups chocolate cereal crumbs

1 tablespoon sugar

2 packets heat-stable artificial sweetener

Melt margarine and combine with all other ingredients in a food processor. Press mixture ¾ inch up sides of the springform and then press and smooth remainder over bottom.

Filling and Garnish

8 ounces imitation cream cheese

8 ounces low-fat cottage cheese, drained well

¼ cup nonfat dry milk

1 teaspoon instant coffee

¾ teaspoon coffee extract

¼ teaspoon vanilla

¼ cup sugar

8 packages heat-stable artificial sweetener

2 large egg whites

1 ounce mocha-flavored chocolate

Blend together all ingredients except for egg whites in food processor until very smooth and creamy. And egg whites. Blend in with 10 on-off pulses. Pour into crust and bake for 30 minutes. Refrigerate. When chilled, grate mocha-flavored chocolate on top.

LOWER-CALORIE NO-BAKE
LEMON-LIME-MINT CHEESECAKE

Coat 8-inch springform pan with vegetable oil spray.

Crust

1/4 cup reduced-fat margarine

1 1/2 cups crumbs from a crunchy sweet cereal

3 packages artificial sweetener

1 tablespoon sugar

1/2 teaspoon cinnamon

Melt margarine. Add to all other ingredients in a food processor and process until thoroughly blended. Press 1″ around sides and sprinkle the remainder over the bottom of the springform.

Filling

1 pound light lowfat cottage cheese

1/3 cup sweetened condensed milk

12 packets artificial sweetener

2 tablespoons fresh lime juice

1 tablespoon fresh lemon juice

1/2 teaspoon lemon extract

1/2 teaspoon lime extract

1 teaspoon dried mint

Blend cottage cheese, sweetened condensed milk, and sweetener in food processor until thoroughly blended and smooth. Add juices to batter along with extracts and mint and whip until well blended. Pour into crust and refrigerate until set.

LOWER-CALORIE NO-BAKE
TROPICAL FRUIT CHEESECAKE

Coat 8-inch springform with vegetable oil spray.

Crust

3½ tablespoons reduced-
fat margarine

1½ cups cereal crumbs
from a sweet, crisp
cereal

1 tablespoon sugar

2 packets artificial
sweetener

Melt margarine. Add to crumbs, sugar, and sweetener in processor and process until well blended. Press up sides and pat down over bottom of springform pan.

Filling

1 pound lowfat cottage
cheese

⅓ cup sweetened
condensed milk

2 teaspoons Fruit Fresh

3 tablespoons tropical
blend juice
concentrate, undiluted

1 tablespoon fresh lemon
juice

½ teaspoon guava extract

½ teaspoon passion fruit
extract

6 packets artificial
sweetener

Blend cottage cheese and sweetened condensed milk together in food processor. Dissolve Fruit Fresh in juices and add to food processor along with extracts and sweetener; blend well to combine. Pour into crust and refrigerate until set.

LOWER-CALORIE ORANGE MOCHA
NO-BAKE CHEESECAKE

Coat 10-inch springform with vegetable oil spray.

Crust

1/4 cup (4 tablespoons) reduced-fat margarine

1 1/2 cups crumbs from a chocolate cereal

1 tablespoon sugar

2 packets artificial sweetener

1/2 teaspoon cinnamon

Melt margarine. Blend thoroughly with crumbs, sugar, sweetener, and cinnamon in food processor. Press mixture 3/4 inch up the sides of the springform, then sprinkle remaining crumbs over bottom of pan.

Filling

1/2 pound imitation cream cheese

1/2 pound part-skim-milk ricotta

1/3 cup sweetened condensed milk

4 teaspoons Fruit Fresh

3 tablespoons frozen orange juice concentrate, undiluted

2 tablespoons cocoa

6 packets artificial sweetener

1 teaspoon mocha extract

Optional Garnish

1 1/2 tablespoon cocoa
1 package artificial sweetener

Blend cheeses and condensed milk in food processor until smooth and creamy. Dissolve Fruit Fresh in orange juice and add to processor with cocoa, sweetener, and mocha extract. Process until well blended. Pour into crust and put into refrigerator to set.

If desired, combine cocoa with sweetener and sprinkle on top of cake for decoration.

LOWER-CALORIE NO-BAKE RASPBERRY DAIQUIRI CHEESECAKE

Coat 8-inch springform pan with vegetable oil spray.

Crust

1/4 cup (4 tablespoons) reduced-fat margarine

1 1/4 cups crumbs from a crunchy, sweet cereal

1 tablespoon sugar

3 packages artificial sweetener

1/2 teaspoon cinnamon

Warm margarine slightly. Add to all other ingredients in a food processor and process until thoroughly blended. Press around sides and sprinkle over bottom of the springform.

Filling

12 ounces dry-flake cottage cheese

4 ounces small curd cottage cheese

1/3 cup sweetened condensed milk

12 packets artificial sweetener

3 tablespoons frozen raspberry daiquiri mix concentrate, undiluted

1 tablespoon lime juice

2 teaspoons Fruit Fresh

1 1/2 cups sweet, fresh raspberries

Process cheeses, sweetened condensed milk, and sweetener in food processor until thoroughly blended and smooth. Dissolve Fruit Fresh in juices, add to batter, and process until well blended. Distribute raspberries over crust, smooth batter over them, and refrigerate until set.

Other Cakes

SOME NOTES ABOUT CAKES

None of the following cakes are layer cakes. Most layer cakes are bland and uninteresting. That's why they're always slathered with icing. Only one of these cakes requires glaze. Just dust the others with confectioners' sugar right before serving.

Cakes should cool in the pan, on racks, or elevated on two similarly sized cans, so that air can get around and under them. The most important pan in this section is a 10- × 4-inch tube pan of professional quality, made of very heavy aluminum, with a center that does not come out. If the pan is well greased and dusted with flour, there will be no problems in removing the cake.

How to Know if Your Cake Is Done

1. E.S.P.
2. Insert a cake tester or a knife into the center of the cake and if it comes out completely clean, the cake is done.
3. Hold the cake up to your ear. If there is any snap, crackle, or popping noise, that means the eggs are still combining

with the other ingredients, and the cake should be baked longer. When the cake is silent, it is done.

A Note for Those Cooks Who are Afraid of Separating Eggs

1. Separate the whites from the yolks when the eggs are cold.
2. Put the egg whites in a warmed mixing bowl.
3. Attach the wire whip to the mixer and begin beating the whites on low speed.
4. When they become frothy, add ⅛ teaspoon of cream of tartar and beat on high speed until they form stiff peaks.

(*Note*: Egg whites are traditionally whipped in a copper bowl; the copper imparts minerals to the egg whites. When you are not using a copper bowl, add cream of tartar to substitute for the missing minerals. Copper bowls that fit into the KitchenAid mixer are available from Atlas Metal Spinning Company, 185 Beacon St., South San Francisco, CA 94080, or from many catalogs.)

5. To fold in remaining batter, add it gradually to the egg whites in the bowl. If using a KitchenAid, the wire whip on the lowest speed will blend them in beautifully.

PINEAPPLE NUT POUND CAKE

¾ cup sugar
3 tablespoons flour
Pinch of salt
¾ cup pineapple juice
3 egg yolks, slightly beaten

2 tablespoons lightly salted butter
½ cup well-drained pineapple chunks

In the top of a double boiler over simmering water combine sugar, flour, and salt. Add pineapple juice and egg yolks. Cook, stirring, until mixture thickens. When thick, add butter and pineapple chunks. Set aside to cool.

2 tablespoons butter, melted

½ cup chopped walnuts

½ cup brown sugar, packed

2 teaspoons cinnamon

2 teaspoons flour

Melt butter, add to nuts, and coat well. Add brown sugar, cinnamon, and flour. Toss well.

Preheat oven to 350° F.
Grease and flour 10- × 4-inch tube pan.

½ pound (2 sticks) lightly salted butter

½ cup vegetable oil

3 cups sugar

6 extra-large eggs

2 teaspoons vanilla extract

1 teaspoon fresh lime juice

3 cups flour

½ teaspoon baking powder

Pinch of salt

1 cup buttermilk

Confectioners' sugar

In a mixer, beat butter, oil, and sugar until fluffy. Add eggs, one at a time, beating well after each addition. Add vanilla and lime juice. Combine flour, baking powder, and salt. Add to batter alternately with buttermilk, beginning and ending with the flour (⅓ flour, ½ buttermilk, ⅓ flour, ½ buttermilk, ⅓ flour). Pour into the prepared pan and bake in preheated oven for 30 minutes. Remove from oven and carefully push pineapple and nut mixtures into already partially baked batter. Return to oven and bake for 50 minutes more, or until a knife or tester inserted in the center of the cake comes out clean. Cool on rack. Sprinkle with confectioners' sugar.

SOUTHERN COCONUT CAKE

Preheat oven to 325° F.
Grease a 10- × 4-inch tube pan,
and line the bottom with parchment paper.

½ pound (2 sticks) lightly salted butter

2 cups sugar

4 large eggs, separated

⅛ teaspoon cream of tartar (if egg whites will not be whipped in a copper bowl)

½ pound white chocolate, melted over simmering water in a double boiler, in a pan on a heat diffuser, or in microwave oven

1 teaspoon vanilla extract

2½ cups flour, sifted

1 teaspoon baking powder

½ teaspoon salt

1 cup skim milk

1 teaspoon lemon juice

1 cup chopped pecans

1 cup grated coconut

Confectioners' sugar

In a food processor, cream butter and sugar. Add egg yolks and cut in. Add chocolate and vanilla and cut in. Sift flour, baking powder, and salt together. Combine milk and lemon juice. Add flour mixture and milk mixture alternately to chocolate mixture, beginning and ending with flour (⅓ flour, ½ milk, ⅓ flour, ½ milk, ⅓ flour). In mixer, whip egg whites with optional cream of tartar until stiff with wire whip. Fold into batter egg whites, pecans, and coconut using wire whip on lowest speed of mixer. Bake for 1 hour and 20 minutes or until a knife or tester inserted in the center comes out clean. Cool for 30 minutes and then turn out on a rack.

Note: The top of this cake tends to crack. Sprinkle with confectioners' sugar.

BRANDIED POUND CAKE

Preheat oven to 325° F.
Butter and flour a 10- × 4-inch tube pan.

1 pound (4 sticks) lightly
    salted butter
3 cups sugar
6 extra-large eggs
3 tablespoons cognac
1 teaspoon mace

3½ cups unsifted flour
¾ cup evaporated milk
    mixed with ¼ cup
    water
Confectioners' sugar

In a mixer, beat the butter and sugar until fluffy and light in color. Add the eggs, one at a time, beating well after each addition. Add cognac and mace. Add flour alternately with milk-water mixture, with flour in three parts and milk-water in two parts (⅓ flour, ½ milk, ⅓ flour, ½ milk, ⅓ flour). Bake in the preheated oven for 2 hours, or until a knife or tester inserted in the center comes out clean. Cool on a rack. Sprinkle with confectioners' sugar.

Note: This cake is best baked the day before serving. Turn it upside-down to serve.

TUTTI-FRUTTI CARROT CAKE

Preheat oven to 325° F.
Butter and flour a 10- × 4-inch tube pan.

1½ cups vegetable oil

2 cups sugar

4 large eggs

1 teaspoon salt

2 cups flour

2 teaspoons baking soda

1 teaspoon cinnamon extract

1½ cups grated carrots (about 1 pound)

½ cup chopped walnuts

½ cup white raisins, soaked in ¼ cup brandy for ½ hour, then carefully drained

½ cup drained crushed pineapple

2 ounces sweet chocolate, grated

Confectioners' sugar

In the mixer, with wire whip attached, cream the oil and sugar. Add the eggs, one at a time, beating well after each addition. Sift together salt, flour, and baking soda. Add to batter and blend. Add cinnamon extract, carrots, walnuts, raisins, pineapple, and chocolate and blend thoroughly.

Pour batter into pan and bake in the preheated oven for 1½ hours, until a knife or tester inserted in the center comes out clean. Cool on rack. Turn cake upside down into serving plate. Before serving sprinkle with confectioners' sugar.

Optional Icing

½ pound (one 8-ounce package) cream cheese, softened

4 tablespoons (½ stick) unsalted butter, melted

1 tablespoon fresh lime juice

½ pound confectioners' sugar

Beat cream cheese until light and fluffy. Gradually add the melted butter, beating until it is completely absorbed. Add lime juice, then add sugar gradually, beating well until the icing is smooth. Spread on cake and refrigerate to set.

POPPYSEED POUND CAKE

Preheat oven to 300° F.
Grease and flour a 10- × 4-inch tube pan.

½ pound (2 sticks) lightly salted butter

3 cups sugar

6 large eggs, separated

¼ teaspoon baking soda

3 cups sifted flour

1 cup sour cream

1 teaspoon fresh lime juice

¼ cup poppyseed pastry filling

½ cup large walnut pieces

⅛ teaspoon cream of tartar (if egg whites are not whipped in copper bowl)

Confectioners' sugar

In a mixer, cream butter and sugar thoroughly. Stir in egg yolks one at a time. Add soda to flour. Add flour mix and sour cream to batter alternately, beginning and ending with flour (⅓ flour, ½ sour cream, ⅓ flour, ½ sour cream, ⅓ flour). Stir in lime juice, poppyseed, and walnuts. In a mixer on high speed, with wire whip, beat egg whites with optional cream of tartar until stiff. Fold into batter with wire whip on lowest speed until completely blended together. Bake for 2 hours and 15 minutes, or until knife or tester inserted in the center comes out clean. Let cool on rack for 30 minutes before taking out of pan. Cake should be served right side up, sprinkled with confectioners' sugar.

WHITE CHOCOLATE CHIP POUND CAKE

Preheat oven to 325° F.
Butter a 10- × 4-inch tube pan.

½ pound (2 sticks) unsalted butter

One 8-ounce package cream cheese

2 cups sugar

1 teaspoon coffee extract

2 teaspoons vanilla extract

4 large eggs

2 teaspoons baking powder

2 cups sifted flour

6 ounces white chocolate, chopped into chip-sized pieces in a food processor

½ cup finely chopped black or English walnuts

Confectioners' sugar

In a mixer, cream butter, cream cheese, and sugar until fluffy, then add the extracts. Add eggs, one at a time, beating well after each addition. Sift together baking powder and flour. Add to batter and beat at medium to high speed until flour is completely incorporated. By hand stir in chocolate bits. Coat prepared pan with nuts. Do sides of pan first (use your hand if necessary to make nuts adhere to sides), then coat bottom of pan with the remaining nuts. Spoon batter into pan and bake in the preheated oven for 1 hour and 20 minutes, or until a knife or tester inserted in the center comes out clean. Cool on rack. Sprinkle with confectioners' sugar.

CHOCOLATE CRIME

Preheat oven to 350° F.
Butter a 13- × 9- × 2-inch pan.

1 cup half-and-half

1 teaspoon raspberry
vinegar

1 teaspoon baking soda

1 teaspoon coffee liqueur

1 cup hot water

1/2 pound (2 sticks) lightly
salted butter, melted

1/4 cup cocoa

2 cups sugar

2 large eggs

2 cups flour

1 teaspoon instant
espresso

This cake may be mixed with a spoon or a whisk. Combine half-and-half, vinegar, baking soda, and coffee liqueur in a bowl and set aside. In another bowl blend the water, butter, and cocoa. Add sugar, then eggs. Combine flour and espresso. Mix flour and half-and-half mixture alternately into batter (1/3 flour, 1/2 half-and-half, 1/3 flour, 1/2 half-and-half, 1/3 flour). Don't worry if batter seems thin and runny. It should be that way. Bake 45 minutes or until a knife or tester inserted in the center comes out clean. Cool on rack.

This is best with a glaze.

Icing

1/2 cup half-and-half

1 teaspoon instant
espresso

6 tablespoons (3/4 stick)
butter

1 cup sugar

8 ounces sweet chocolate,
in chip-sized pieces

In a saucepan, scald half-and-half and espresso. Then add all at once butter, sugar, and chips. Bring to a boil. Pour over hot cake.

GINGER CAKE

Preheat oven to 350° F.
Butter and flour a 10- × 4-inch tube pan.

½ cup crystallized ginger, chopped in a food processor

¼ cup brandy

2 cups flour

½ pound (2 sticks) lightly salted butter

1 cup sugar

6 large eggs

2 teaspoons ground ginger

½ cup chopped walnuts

Confectioners' sugar

Soak crystallized ginger in brandy overnight, then drain, reserving brandy. Add ½ cup of the flour to the ginger and stir well. To the brandy remaining, add enough additional brandy to equal ¼ cup. Beat butter until fluffy. Add sugar and beat until well combined. Add eggs, one at a time, beating well after each addition. Mix the remaining 1½ cups flour with ground ginger. Mix flour into cake. Add brandy, nuts, and the ginger. Mix until well distributed. Bake for 60 minutes or until a knife or tester inserted in the center comes out clean. Cool on rack. This cake does not rise a great deal. It is dense, and should be thinly sliced. Sprinkle with confectioners' sugar.

CRANBERRY NUT TORTE

Preheat oven to 350° F.

Crust

2 cups finely chopped walnuts

2 tablespoons lightly salted butter, melted

2 tablespoons sugar

Combine ingredients in food processor and press over bottom and halfway up sides of a 10-inch springform pan.

Filling

1 cup sugar

3/4 cup flour

1/4 pound (1 stick) lightly salted butter, melted

2 large eggs

1 1/2 teaspoons almond extract

8 ounces fresh or frozen whole cranberries

1/2 cup coarsely chopped walnuts

Confectioners' sugar

In a bowl, combine flour and sugar. Reserve. Using the whisk attachment of a mixer, combine butter, eggs, and almond extract. Mix in flour and sugar. With a rubber spatula, fold in cranberries and walnuts. Pour into springform pan. Bake in preheated oven for 1 hour and 5 minutes, or until a knife or tester inserted in the center comes out clean. Cool on rack. Sprinkle heavily with confectioners' sugar.

CALVADOS CAKE

Preheat oven to 350° F.
Line a 9- × 13- or 11- × 11-inch pan with parchment paper.

1/2 cup calvados or applejack

4 large apples, peeled, cored, and coarsely chopped (about 4 cups)

1 cup chopped walnuts

1 cup white raisins

2 cups flour

1/2 cup vegetable oil

2 cups sugar

2 eggs

2 teaspoons cinnamon

1 teaspoon nutmeg

1/2 teaspoon ground cloves

1 teaspoon salt

2 teaspoons baking soda

Pour calvados over apples. Mix in walnuts, raisins, and flour. In a separate bowl, combine the remaining ingredients and blend thoroughly. Combine with apple mixture. Pour into the lined pan. Bake in preheated oven for 1 hour, or until knife or tester inserted in the center comes out clean. Cool on rack.

SUPER CHOCOLATEY CAKE

Preheat oven to 350° F.
Butter and flour a 10- × 4-inch tube pan.

1 cup vegetable oil
3 cups sugar
3 large eggs
1 tablespoon vanilla
   extract
6 ounces unsweetened
   chocolate, melted
2 cups hot coffee

3 cups flour
1 tablespoon baking
   powder
½ teaspoon salt
1½ cups sweet chocolate,
   chopped to chips in
   the food processor
Confectioners' sugar

Beat together the oil and sugar. Add the eggs, one at a time, beating well after each addition. Add vanilla and melted chocolate. Add coffee and blend thoroughly. Combine flour, baking powder, and salt, then incorporate into batter. Fold in chocolate chips. Bake in preheated oven for 1½ hours, or until knife or tester inserted in the center comes out clean. Cool on rack. Sprinkle with confectioners' sugar.

ORANGE GLAZE CAKE

Preheat oven to 350° F.
Butter and flour a 10- × 4-inch tube pan.

Cake

¼ pound (1 stick) lightly salted butter

¼ pound (1 stick) margarine

2 cups sugar

½ teaspoon vanilla extract

5 large eggs

3 cups cake flour

1 tablespoon baking powder

½ teaspoon salt

¾ cup milk

2 tablespoons grated orange rind

Confectioners' sugar

Cream shortening, sugar, and vanilla in a mixer. Add eggs, one at a time, beating well after each addition. Sift cake flour, baking powder, and salt together. Mix flour mixture and milk alternately into batter (⅓ flour, ½ milk, ⅓ flour, ½ milk, ⅓ flour). Fold in rind. Bake in tube pan in preheated oven for 1 hour and 10 minutes, or until knife or tester inserted in the center comes out clean. Sprinkle with confectioners' sugar.

Glaze

4 tablespoons (½ stick) lightly salted butter

⅔ cup sugar

⅓ cup orange juice

While cake bakes, simmer glaze ingredients in a saucepan for 5 minutes and let cool. When cake is done, cool on rack for 10 minutes. Poor cool glaze over warm cake while cake is still in the pan, and let stand for 30 minutes. Turn out and serve.

Holiday Treats

Notes about Cookies

All of these cookies are easy to make. They all taste spectacular. They make perfect gifts for anyone whose taste buds you respect. There is one problem: if you don't live alone, they usually don't keep long enough for you to give them away unless you hide them where hungry kids or adults can't find them. The cookies should be stored in tins that have been lined with *wax paper*, not plastic wrap. The tins should be hidden in the darkest broom closet or attic, where humans rooting around for sweets will never think of looking. My son wouldn't be caught dead in the broom closet lest I suggest he sweep the floor. If your children are more helpful, then they deserve to find the treats.

If you hate to clean cookie sheets, line them with parchment paper, which browns baked goods yet doesn't end up, as foil can, between your teeth.

I prefer fresh, grated coconut in the following cookie recipes, but I know that's hard to come by. Acceptable substitutes are unsweetened dried coconut (found in health food stores) or the sweetened dried coconut always available in supermarkets.

MINCEMEAT SQUARES

Preheat oven to 350° F.
Line a 9- × 9-inch pan with buttered parchment paper.

1½ cups regular rolled oats

1½ cups flour

1½ cups light brown sugar, firmly packed

½ teaspoon salt

1 teaspoon cinnamon

¼ pound + 4 tablespoons (1½ sticks) unsalted butter

1 pound mincemeat (I prefer fresh mincemeat, which is usually available during the holiday season; if canned mincemeat is used, ¼ cup brandy to contents of jar and let it sit overnight before using)

½ cup (2 ounces) chopped walnuts

In a food processor, combine oats, flour, sugar, salt, cinnamon, and butter. Pat two-thirds of mixture in bottom of baking pan. Spread mincemeat over mixture. Combine nuts with remaining oat mixture and sprinkle on top. Bake in preheated oven 40 minutes. Cool. Cut into 1½-inch squares. Makes 3 dozen.

PECAN SANDIES

Preheat oven to 325°F.

½ pound (2 sticks) unsalted butter

⅓ cup sugar

1 tablespoon water

1 teaspoon vanilla extract

2 cups flour

1 cup (4 ounces) finely chopped pecans

Confectioners' sugar to roll baked cookies in

In a mixer, cream butter with sugar. Add water, vanilla, flour, and nuts and beat until blended. Roll into finger shapes. Place 1 inch apart on ungreased cookie sheets. Bake in preheated oven for 20 minutes. Remove carefully to rack. When cool roll in confectioners' sugar. Makes 6 dozen.

WALNUT PUFFS

Preheat oven to 300°F.

½ pound (2 sticks) unsalted butter

½ cup confectioners' sugar, plus confectioners' sugar to roll puffs in

1 teaspoon vanilla extract

2 cups sifted flour

1 cup (4 ounces) finely chopped walnuts

In a mixer, cream butter. Add ½ cup confectioners' sugar and vanilla and blend until creamy. Add flour and combine. Add nuts and mix. Roll into balls about 1½ to 2 inches in diameter. Place 1 inch apart on ungreased cookie sheet. Bake in preheated oven for 15 minutes. Roll hot puffs in confectioners' sugar. Let cook on racks. Then roll puffs again in confectioners' sugar. Makes 4 dozen.

MAGIC BARS

Preheat oven to 350° F.
Line a 9- × 13-inch baking pan with buttered parchment paper.

¼ pound + 2 tablespoons (1¼ sticks) unsalted butter

2 cups crushed cornflakes

1 can (about 1⅓ cups) sweetened condensed milk

1 cup miniature chocolate chips

1 cup grated coconut

1 cup (4 ounces) finely chopped walnuts

Melt butter. Mix with cornflakes. Pat mixture evenly over bottom of pan. Drizzle condensed milk evenly over crumbs. Sprinkle on chips, coconut, and nuts. Press down gently. Bake in preheated oven for 30 minutes, or until golden brown. Cool. Cut into 1½-inch squares. Makes 4 dozen.

COCO PECAN SQUARES

Preheat oven to 350° F
Butter a 9- × 9-inch pan.

¼ pound (1 stick) lightly salted butter

½ cup dark brown sugar, firmly packed

1 cup plus 2 tablespoons flour

2 large eggs

1 cup light brown sugar

1 cup coarsely chopped pecans

½ cup grated coconut

1 teaspoon vanilla extract

Pinch of salt

In a mixer, cream butter and dark brown sugar. Add 1 cup flour and blend thoroughly. Press into pan, spreading out into corners. Bake in preheated oven for 20 minutes.

Beat eggs with light brown sugar until thick. Add pecans. Toss coconut with 2 tablespoons flour and combine, along with vanilla and salt. Mix well. Spread topping over crust. Bake for 20 minutes longer. Let cool and cut into squares. Makes 4 dozen.

POUND CAKE WAFERS

Preheat oven to 400° F.
Butter cookie sheets.

½ pound (2 sticks) butter
1 cup sugar
2 large eggs, beaten

2 cups flour
1½ teaspoons nutmeg or mace

In a mixer, cream the butter and sugar very well. Add eggs. Sift flour and nutmeg several times and add to batter. Mix well. Drop by teaspoonfuls on cookie sheets, but not too close together as the cookies spread while baking. Pat down with the back of a teaspoon that has been dipped in flour. Bake in preheated oven for about 6 minutes. Cool on rack. Makes 5 dozen.

VANILLA CHIP COOKIES

Preheat oven to 350° F.
Butter cookie sheets.

½ pound (2 sticks) lightly salted butter

⅔ cup sugar

1 large egg

2 teaspoons vanilla extract

2½ cups flour

½ teaspoon baking powder

6 ounces white chocolate, chopped in food processor into chip-sized pieces

In a mixer, cream butter and sugar until fluffy. Add egg and vanilla. Sift flour with baking powder and mix in. Stir in chips by hand. Drop by teaspoonfuls on cookie sheets, 2 inches apart. Don't pat down. It should be a mounded cookie. Bake in preheated oven for 12 minutes. Cool on rack. Makes 6 dozen.

PEANUT BUTTER COOKIES

Preheat oven to 350° F.
Butter cookie sheets.

½ pound (2 sticks) lightly salted butter

2 cups brown sugar, firmly packed

2 large eggs

1 cup peanut butter

3 cups flour

2 teaspoons baking soda

5 dozen peanut halves

In a mixer, cream butter and sugar. Add eggs, then peanut butter, beating until well incorporated into batter. Sift flour with baking soda and mix in. Refrigerate until dough may be handled easily, about 1 hour. Roll dough into small balls about 1 inch in diameter. Place on cookie sheets 3 inches apart. Flatten with a fork, once each way, to make a crisscross design. Press peanut half into the center of each cookie and bake in preheated oven for 20 minutes. Cool in rack. Makes 5 dozen.

IRISH LACE COOKIES

Preheat oven to 350° F.
Butter cookie sheets.

3 large eggs
³/4 teaspoon salt
1¹/₃ cups sugar
1¹/₂ tablespoons lightly salted butter, melted
1 teaspoon coffee liqueur
¹/4 teaspoon coffee extract
¹/4 teaspoon vanilla extract

¹/4 teaspoon grated nutmeg
1 tablespoon plus 1 teaspoon baking powder
3¹/₂ cups uncooked quick-cooking oatmeal
¹/₂ cup (2 ounces) chopped nuts (optional)

In a mixer, beat eggs well with salt. Add sugar gradually. Then stir in remaining ingredients on lowest speed of mixer. Drop by teaspoonfuls onto cookie sheets, about a dozen to a sheet, because they tend to spread. Bake in preheated oven for 10 minutes, or until a delicate brown. Remove from pans at once and place on racks to cool. Makes about 5 dozen.

PEAR SQUARES

Preheat oven to 350° F.
Line an 8- × 8-inch pan with buttered parchment paper.

2 cups dried pears, finely
  chopped in food
  processor
1 cup light brown sugar,
  firmly packed
1 cup water
1 cup + 1 tablespoon
  flour

1 teaspoon vanilla extract
1 teaspoon baking soda
2 cups cornflakes
1/4 pound + 4 tablespoons
  (1 1/2 sticks) lightly
  salted butter, melted

Cook pears, 1/2 cup of the sugar, water, and 1 tablespoon of the flour in a saucepan until thick, and reserve off heat. Combine the remaining ingredients. Spread half of the flour mixture in pan. Cover with pear sauce and spread the rest of the flour mixture on top. Bake in preheated oven 20 minutes. Cool. Remove from pan and cut into squares. Makes about 2 dozen large or 4 dozen small squares.

ALVIN'S DELIGHT

Preheat oven to 350° F.
Line an 8- × 8-inch pan with parchment paper.

Crust

1/4 pound (1 stick) lightly
  salted butter

1/2 cup light brown sugar,
  firmly packed
1 cup sifted flour

In a mixer, cream butter, then add sugar and flour, blending thoroughly. Spread about ¼ inch thick on pan. Bake in preheated oven for 10 minutes. While crust is baking, prepare topping. When crust is done, increase oven temperature to 375°F.

Topping

2 large eggs

½ cup light brown sugar, firmly packed

1 teaspoon coffee liqueur

2 tablespoons flour

½ teaspoon baking powder

¼ teaspoon salt

½ cup chopped Brazil nuts

½ cup butterscotch bits

½ cup peanut butter chips

½ cup chopped white chocolate

1 cup grated coconut

In a mixer, beat eggs, then add sugar and coffee liqueur and beat until light and fluffy. Sift flour, baking powder, and salt together. Add to egg mixture. Add nuts, butterscotch bits, chocolate, and ½ cup of the coconut. Mix thoroughly with egg mixture. Pour over baked crust. Sprinkle with the remaining ½ cup coconut. Bake in preheated oven for 25 minutes, or until topping is firm. Cut into squares when partially cool. These are very rich so small squares are quite adequate. Makes about 5 dozen.

CINNAMON STRIPS

Preheat oven to 350° F.
Butter an 11- × 15- × 3/4-inch cookie sheet.

1/2 pound (2 sticks) lightly
    salted butter

3/4 cup sugar

2 cups flour

1 egg, separated

1 tablespoon plus 1
    teaspoon cinnamon

1 teaspoon sherry extract
    or sherry

1 cup chopped pecans

Confectioners' sugar

Cream butter and sugar. Gradually add flour, then egg yolk, cinnamon, and extract. Pat down in prepared pan until about 1/4 inch thick all over. With a brush spread the unbeaten egg white all over the top, then press chopped pecans down into batter. Bake in preheated oven for 30 minutes. Cut into oblong pieces while hot. When cool dip in confectioners' sugar. They are delicious in 1-inch × 3-inch fingers. Makes about 3 dozen.

BLOND BROWNIES

Preheat oven to 350° F.
Line an 8- × 8-inch pan with parchment paper.

2 large eggs
1 cup sugar
1/4 pound (1 stick) lightly salted butter, melted
2 ounces white chocolate, melted in a double boiler over simmering water, in a pan on a heat diffuser, or in a microwave oven
3/4 cup sifted flour
1 cup finely chopped Brazil nuts
1 teaspoon coffee liqueur
1/4 teaspoon coffee extract
Confectioners' sugar

In a mixer, beat eggs slightly, add sugar, and stir. Add butter and white chocolate and beat in on lowest speed of mixer. Combine flour and nuts and add to egg mixture. Add coffee liqueur and coffee extract, beating until well blended on the lowest speed of the mixer. Pour into pan. Bake in preheated oven for 35 minutes. Cool and cut into 1- × 2-inch fingers. Roll in confectioners' sugar. Makes about 2½ dozen.

FRUITCAKE DROPS

Preheat oven to 300° F.
Butter cookie sheets.

2 tablespoons lightly
salted butter

5 tablespoons brown
sugar, firmly packed

2 tablespoons ginger
marmalade

1 large egg

1 teaspoon baking soda

1¾ teaspoons brandy

¾ cup flour

¼ teaspoon allspice

¼ teaspoon ground cloves

¼ teaspoon cinnamon

¼ teaspoon ground
nutmeg

2 cups chopped pecans

½ pound golden raisins

¼ pound dried papaya,
chopped in food
processor

¼ pound dried pineapple,
chopped in food
processor

¼ pound dried California
apricots, chopped in
food processor

In a mixer, cream butter. Add sugar, marmalade, and egg, blending thoroughly. Dissolve baking soda in brandy and add to creamed mixture on the lowest setting of mixer. Sift the flour with spices. Gradually add half to butter mixture. Dredge nuts and fruits in remaining flour and stir into batter. Mix well. Drop by teaspoonfuls onto cookie sheets. Bake in preheated oven for 18 minutes. These cookies will ripen like fruitcakes. Makes 5 dozen.

SHORTBREAD SURPRISE

Preheat oven to 325° F.

4 ounces dried apricots

1 pound (4 sticks) lightly salted butter

4 cups flour

1 teaspoon salt

3/4 cup confectioners' sugar

1 teaspoon nutmeg

1 1/4 cups (4 ounces) grated coconut

Chop apricots in food processor and cover with boiling water for 5 minutes. Drain water and place softened apricots on paper towels. In a mixer, cream butter. Beat in flour, salt, sugar, and nutmeg on lowest speed of mixer until well combined. Place in an ungreased 11- × 15- × 3/4-inch pan and spread around and pat down so batter is about 1/2 inch thick. Spread apricots over top of batter. Sprinkle coconut over apricots and press into dough. Bake in preheated oven for 45 minutes. While hot, cut into whatever shapes you desire. Yield depends on shape.

BRANDY SNAPS

Preheat oven to 350° F.

4 tablespoons (1/2 stick) lightly salted butter

1/4 cup sugar

2 tablespoons imported golden sugar syrup

1/2 cup unbleached flour

1/2 teaspoon ginger extract

1 teaspoon Grand Marnier

1 tablespoon grated orange rind

Confectioners' sugar for sprinkling

Cream butter and sugar. Add the remaining ingredients and mix thoroughly but gently. Drop by half-teaspoonfuls on cookie sheets and bake in preheated oven for about 7 minutes, or until golden brown. Bake only a dozen on a sheet, as they spread. As soon as you can lift them off the pan, remove them. While they are still warm and pliable, fold each one around your finger so they become shaped like a taco. Sprinkle with confectioners' sugar before serving. If they overcook a little and get a deep brown, don't worry about them. Serve them flat, sprinkled with lots of confectioners' sugar (it hides all the imperfections). Makes about 4 dozen.

DARK RUM BALLS

1½ cups finely ground chocolate cookie crumbs

½ cup confectioners' sugar

¾ cup finely ground blanched almonds

1¾ teaspoons cocoa

2 tablespoons light corn syrup

½ cup dark rum

Confectioners' sugar for rolling

Combine all the ingredients thoroughly and form into small balls. Roll in confectioners' sugar and wrap in aluminum foil to mellow. Makes about 3 dozen.

LUSCIOUS LIME SQUARES

Preheat oven to 350° F.
Butter parchment paper to cover bottom and
sides of an 8- × 12- × 2-inch pan.

One 15-ounce can
sweetened condensed
milk
½ cup fresh lime juice
1½ teaspoons grated lime
rind
1½ cups sifted
unbleached flour
1 teaspoon baking powder
½ teaspoon salt

1 teaspoon ground ginger
11 tablespoons (1 stick
plus 3 tablespoons)
lightly salted butter
¾ cup dark brown sugar,
firmly packed
1 cup uncooked quick-
cooking oatmeal
½ cup finely chopped
pecans

Blend together milk, lime juice, and rind and set aside. Sift together
flour, baking powder, salt, and ginger. In mixer, cream butter and
blend in sugar. Add oatmeal, flour mixture, and nuts and beat on
lowest speed of mixer until crumbly. Spread about half of the flour
mixture in the prepared pan and pat down. Spread condensed milk
mixture over top of flour mixture and sprinkle remaining crumbs on
top of everything. Bake in preheated oven for about 25 minutes, or
until brown around edges. Cool in pan for about 15 minutes at room
temperature, then refrigerate until firm. Remove from pan and cut
into 1¾-inch squares. These cookies should be refrigerated until 1
hour before serving. Makes about 2½ dozen.

THE SUPERJUNK SQUARE

Preheat oven to 325° F.
Line an 8- × 8-inch pan with parchment paper.

¼ pound (1 stick) lightly salted butter

½ cup dark brown sugar

1 cup sifted unbleached flour

Combine butter, sugar, and flour. Spread about ¼ inch thick on lined pan and bake at 325° F for 10 minutes. Remove from oven and increase oven temperature to 375° F.

2 large eggs

¾ cup dark brown sugar, firmly packed

1 teaspoon coffee liqueur

2 tablespoons flour

½ teaspoon baking powder

¼ teaspoon salt

¾ cup grated coconut

½ cup chopped hazelnuts (filberts)

½ cup butterscotch bits

½ cup milk chocolate chips

½ cup peanut butter chips

Beat eggs, then add sugar and coffee liqueur, and beat until light and fluffy. Sift flour, baking powder, and salt together. Add ½ cup of the coconut, nuts, bits, and chips to flour mixture and combine. Stir in egg mixture and mix thoroughly on low speed of mixer. Spread mixture evenly over top of baked crust and sprinkle with the remaining ¼ cup coconut. Bake at 375°F for 20 minutes, or until top is firm. Cool. Cut into 1-inch squares while still somewhat warm. These are very rich and sweet. Kids love them. Makes about 4 dozen.

TROPICAL TREATS

Preheat oven to 275° F.
Line a 10- × 12- × 2-inch pan
with parchment paper.

1 cup sugar

1⅛ teaspoons baking powder

1 cup + 2 tablespoons unbleached flour

½ teaspoon salt

1½ cups dried papaya, chopped fine in food processor

5 tablespoons finely chopped candied ginger

1½ cups chopped pecans

3 large eggs, separated

⅛ teaspoon cream of tartar (if egg whites are not whipped in copper bowl)

Confectioners' sugar for rolling

Sift together sugar, baking powder, flour, and salt. Combine with papaya, ginger, and nuts. In a mixer, with wire whip, beat egg whites and optional cream of tartar until they form stiff peaks. Beat egg yolks in separate bowl and stir flour mixture into yolks. Fold in egg whites, using the wire whip of mixer on lowest speed. Press evenly into pan. Bake in the preheated oven for 20 minutes. While hot, cut into 1-inch squares and roll into balls at once (some of the cookie may stick to your hands, and you'll have to rinse off with hot water from time to time). Roll balls in confectioners' sugar. Makes about 5 dozen.

COCONUT KISSES

Preheat oven to 300° F.
Butter cookie sheets.

¾ cup sweetened
condensed milk

½ pound grated coconut

½ teaspoon pineapple
extract

1 cup chopped Brazil nuts

2 ounces white chocolate,
chopped

Combine all the ingredients and drop by teaspoonfuls onto well-buttered cookie sheets. Bake in preheated oven for 12 minutes. Cool on racks. Makes 4 dozen.

WALNUT FINGERS

Preheat oven to 275° F.
Line a 10- × 15- × ⅜-inch pan with
buttered parchment paper.

6 large egg whites

⅛ teaspoon cream of
tartar (if egg whites are
not whipped in a
copper bowl)

2 cups cake flour, sifted

⅛ teaspoon salt

1 teaspoon baking powder

1 pound brown sugar,
sifted

3 cups chopped walnuts

1 tablespoon Drambuie

Beat egg whites until they begin to foam, using the wire whip of the mixer at the highest speed, then add cream of tartar (if whites are not whipped in copper bowl) and continue beating till the whites stand up in peaks. Sift flour, salt, and baking powder together. Add brown sugar and mix until combined. Reserve ½ cup of the mixture and dredge walnuts in it. Fold the rest into the egg whites on lowest speed of mixer with wire whip. Fold in walnuts dredged in flour and Drambuie. Spread over pan. Bake in the preheated oven for 60 minutes. When cool cut into fingers. Makes about 4 dozen.

BLACK WALNUT BRANDY BROWNIES

Preheat oven to 325° F.
Line a 10- × 15- × ¾-inch baking pan
with buttered parchment paper.

1 pound black walnuts, chopped

8 ounces unsweetened chocolate

½ pound (2 sticks) unsalted butter

8 large eggs

½ teaspoon salt

4 cups sugar

1 teaspoon vanilla

¼ cup brandy

2 cups flour

Confectioners' sugar for sprinkling

Toast black walnuts and set aside. Melt chocolate and butter in top of double boiler over simmering water, in a saucepan over a heat diffuser, or in microwave oven. Set aside. In a mixer, beat eggs until fluffy. Add salt, sugar, vanilla, and brandy and blend. Add chocolate mixture, flour, and toasted nuts. Mix. Spread in pan and bake in preheated oven for 45 minutes. Let cool. Cut into 1½-inch squares. Sprinkle with confectioners' sugar. Makes 5 dozen.

DROP SAND TARTS

Preheat oven to 375° F.
Butter cookie sheets.

¼ pound (1 stick)
   unsalted butter
1 cup sugar, plus
   additional for
   sprinkling

2 large eggs
1¼ cups sifted flour
1 teaspoon baking powder
Freshly grated nutmeg

Optional

Nuts, finely chopped, for sprinkling

Cream butter and sugar. Add 1 egg. Combine flour and baking powder. Add to batter and mix well. Drop by half teaspoonfuls 2 inches apart on cookie sheet. Beat remaining egg. Flatten cookies very thin with fork dipped into beaten egg. Sprinkle with sugar and nutmeg, and with finely chopped nuts if you like. Bake in preheated oven 10 to 12 minutes. Remove from cookie sheets and cool on racks. Makes 6 to 7 dozen.

CARMELITAS

Preheat oven to 350° F.
Line a 9- × 9-inch pan
with buttered parchment paper.

1½ cups flour

1½ cups rolled oats

1 cup light brown sugar, firmly packed

¾ teaspoon baking soda

Pinch of salt

¼ pound (1 stick) unsalted butter

1 cup miniature chocolate chips

½ cup chopped walnuts

4 tablespoons caramel topping

In a food processor or by hand combine flour, oats, sugar, soda, salt, and butter until mixture is the texture of cornmeal. Press half of mixture over bottom of pan. Bake in preheated oven for 10 minutes. Sprinkle chips, walnuts, and caramel over baked base. Press remaining oat mixture on top and bake for 25 minutes longer. Cool and cut into 1½-inch squares. Makes 3 dozen.

CHRISTMAS BONUS
GEORGIA MOON EGGNOG

8 large eggs

3/4 teaspoon salt

1 cup sugar

1 cup Georgia Moon corn
liquor or bourbon

1/2 cup dark rum

1 quart heavy cream

Nutmeg for garnish

Beat eggs until foamy. Add salt, sugar, and liquors. Mix together. In a separate bowl, lightly whip cream. Fold everything together and let season in refrigerator for a day or two. Stir and serve in stem goblets with fresh nutmeg grated on top. Serves 12 to 16.

Index